GW01524249

TOWER AIR FR COOKBOOK UK

1200 days of Crispy, Delicious and Fast &Easy to Fry, Bake, Grill Recipes for Your Tower Air Fryer

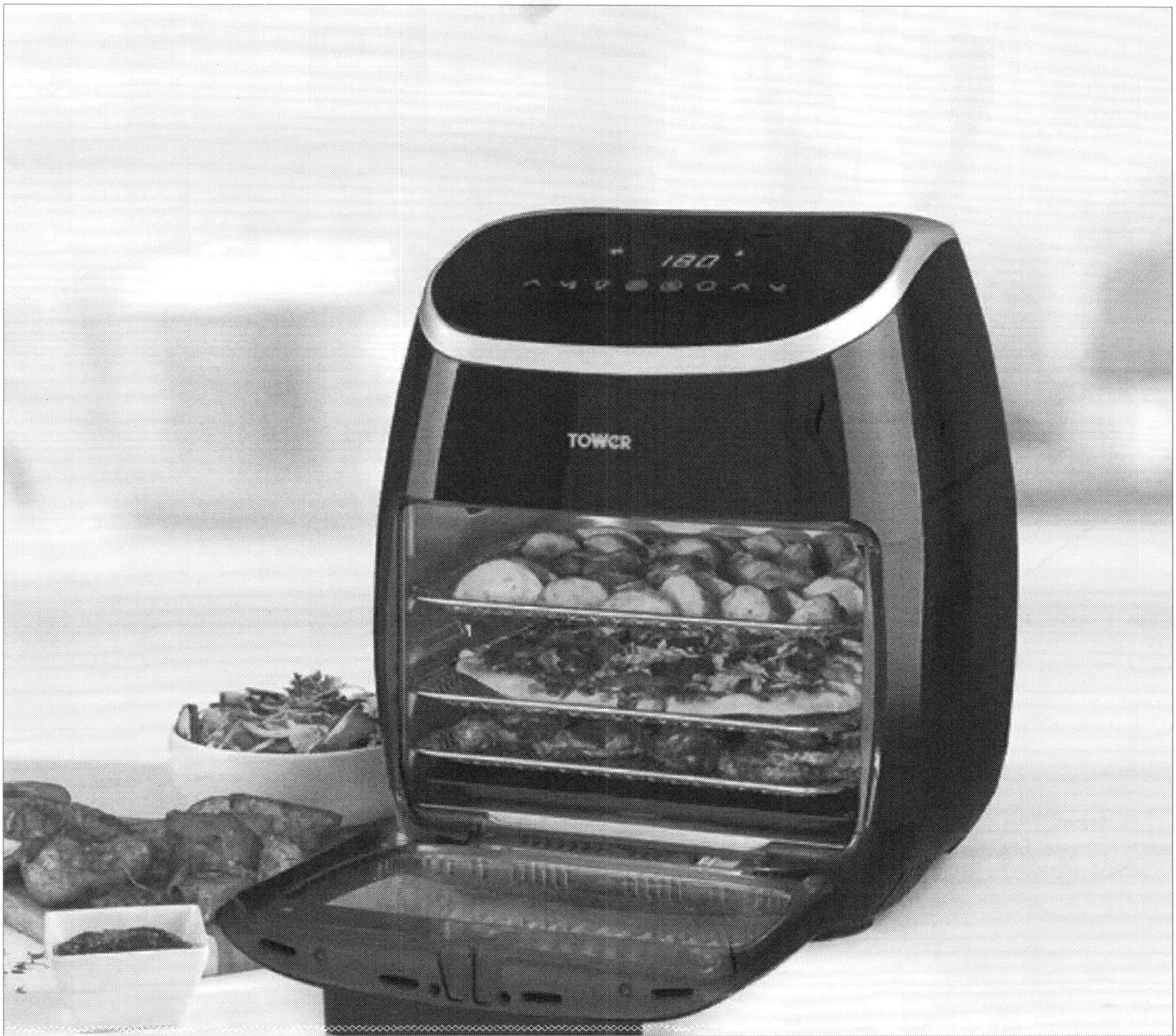

ASHLEY C. SPRADLIN

Copyright© 2022 By Ashley C. Spradlin Rights Reserved

This book is copyright protected. It is only for personal use. You cannot amend, distribute, sell, use, quote or paraphrase any part of the content within this book, without the consent of the author or publisher.

Under no circumstances will any blame or legal responsibility be held against the publisher, or author, for any damages, reparation, or monetary loss due to the information contained within this book, either directly or indirectly.

Disclaimer Notice:

Please note the information contained within this document is for educational and entertainment purposes only. All effort has been executed to present accurate, up to date, reliable, complete information. No warranties of any kind are declared or implied. Readers acknowledge that the author is not engaged in the rendering of legal, financial, medical or professional advice. The content within this book has been derived from various sources. Please consult a licensed professional before attempting any techniques outlined in this book.

By reading this document, the reader agrees that under no circumstances is the author responsible for any losses, direct or indirect, that are incurred as a result of the use of the information contained within this document, including, but not limited to, errors, omissions, or inaccuracies.

Table of Contents

Introduction	1
Chapter 1	
Basics of Tower Air Fryer	2
What is An Air Fryer?	3
Air Fryers Are An Upgrade on Deep Fryers	4
Cleaning the Air Fryer	4
Chapter 2	
Starters and Snacks	5
Ham and Cheese Stuffed Peppers	6
Coriander and Onion Pakoras	6
Italian Rice Balls	7
Panko- Crusted Artichoke Bites	7
Wax Beans with Cumin	8
Spicy Corn Tortilla Chips	8
Turkey Bacon-Wrapped Dates	9
Aubergine with Paprika	9
Olive Nuggets	10
Cheese Stuffed Mushrooms	10
Veggie Prawn Toast	11
Breaded Green Tomatoes with Horseradish	11
Chile Pork Ribs	12
Baked Sardines with Tomato Sauce	12
Broiled Prosciutto-Wrapped Pears	13
Browned Ricotta with Capers and Lemon	13
Bruschetta with Tomato and Basil	14
Roasted Grapes with Yogurt	14
Chapter 3	
Breakfast	15
Soft Pita Breads	16
Tomato-Avocado Toast	16
Turkey-Mushroom Burger	17
Vegan Sandwich-Tofu with Cabbage	17
Muffins with Pecans and Kiwi	18
Sweet Raisins Bread	18
Vanilla-flavour Cherry Scones	19
Easy Deep-Fry Potatoes	19
Buttered Eggs in Bread Hole	20
Egg Pepper Rings with Cherry Tomatoes	20
Parmesan Ranch Onion Risotto	21
Parmesan Egg and banger Muffins	21
Mozzarella Pepperoni Pizza	22
Blueberry Muffins	22
Brown Rice Porridge with Coconut and Dates	22
Chapter 4	
Poultry	23
Gai Yang Chicken	24
Smoked Paprika Chicken	24
Almond Meatballs	25
Sweet Chicken Wings	25
Parmesan and Dill Chicken	26
Ginger and Coconut Chicken	26
Lemon Chicken Thighs	27
Basil Chicken Wings	27
Lemon and Chili Chicken Drumsticks	28
BBQ Wings	28
Garlic Chicken Wings	29
Coriander Chicken Drumsticks	29
Asparagus Chicken	30
Nutmeg Chicken Fillets	30
Chicken and Rice Casserole	31
Lemon Parmesan Chicken	31
Lime Chicken Breasts with Coriander	32
Ground Chicken with Tomatoes	32
Crispy Chicken Strips	33
Chicken with Veggie Couscous Salad	33
Chapter 5	
Beef lamb and Pork	34
Crusted Pork Chops	35
Beef Burger	35
Classic Roast Beef	36
Roast Beef Steaks	36
Air Fried Flank Steak	37
Cheesy Flank Steak	37
Beef with Leeks	38
Beef banger with Tomato Bowl	38
Cheese Steak with Lettuce	39
Courgette Noodle with Beef Meatball	39
Ribs with Chimichurri Sauce	40
Beef Paprika	40
Breaded Pork Loin Chops	41
Pork and Veggie Kebabs	41
Pork and Pineapple Kebabs	42
Bacon-Wrapped Pork Hot Dogs	42
BBQ Kielbasa banger	43
Chapter 6	
Fish and Seafood	44
Honey-Glazed Cod with Sesame Seeds	45
Almond-Lemon Crusted Fish	45
Almond-Coconut Flounder Fillets	46
Lemon-Caper Salmon Burgers	46
Italian-Style Salmon Patties	47
Old Bay Salmon Patty Bites	47
Garlic-Lemon Prawn	48
Trout Amandine with Lemon Butter Sauce	48
Parmesan Sriracha Tuna Patty Sliders	49
Paprika Tilapia with Garlic Aioli	49
Mediterranean Baked Fish Fillet	50
Curried jewfish Fillets with Parmesan	50
Breaded Crab Cakes	51
Flounder Fillet and Asparagus Rolls	51
Stuffed Tilapia with Pepper and Cucumber	52

Chapter 7
Side Dishes — 53
- Air Fried Easy French chips — 54
- Air Fried Bok Choy — 54
- Brussels Sprout with Toasted Pecan — 55
- Balsamic Brussels Sprout with Bacon — 55
- Roasted Cauliflower Florets — 56
- Bacon-Wrapped Asparagus — 56
- Kohlrabi chips — 57
- Air Fry Sweet Potato chips — 57
- Crispy Runner Beans — 58
- Barbecue Parmesan Chicken Nuggets — 58
- Chili Bacon-Wrapped Cabbage Bites — 59
- Cheesy Asparagus — 59
- Air Fried Breaded Mushrooms — 60
- Courgette Fritters — 60
- Air Fried courgette Salad — 61
- Air fryer courgette Chips — 61
- Cauliflower with Lime Juice — 62
- Double Cheese Roasted Asparagus — 62
- Golden Potato, Carrot and Onion — 63
- Potato Shells with Cheddar and Bacon — 63
- Butternut marrow and Parsnip with Thyme — 64
- Ginger-Pepper Broccoli — 64

Chapter 8
Casseroles, Frittata, and Quiche — 65
- Broccoli, Carrot, and Tomato Quiche — 66
- Burgundy Beef and Mushroom Casserole — 66
- Cauliflower and Pumpkin Casserole — 67
- Chicken Divan — 67
- Chicken Ham Casserole — 68
- Chicken banger and Broccoli Casserole — 68
- Chorizo, Corn, and Potato Frittata — 69
- Goat Cheese and Asparagus Frittata — 69
- Riced Cauliflower Casserole — 70
- Banger and Colourful Peppers Casserole — 70
- Prawn Spinach Frittata — 71
- Smoked Trout and Crème Fraiche Frittata — 71
- Spinach and Chickpea Casserole — 72
- Cauliflower Casserole with Pecan Butter — 72
- Cheddar Chicken banger Casserole — 73
- Corn Casserole with Bell Pepper — 73
- Asparagus Casserole with corn meal — 74
- Cheddar Broccoli Casserole — 74
- Tilapia and Rockfish Casserole — 74
- Blueberry and Peach Galette — 75
- Breaded Bananas with Chocolate Sauce — 75

Chapter 9
Desserts — 76
- Caramelized Fruit Kebabs — 77
- Caramelized Pear Tart — 77
- Peach-Blueberry Tart — 78
- Peanut Butter-Chocolate Bread Pudding — 78
- Pumpkin Pudding and Vanilla Wafers — 79
- Strawberry and Rhubarb Crumble — 79
- Summer Berry Crisp — 80
- Vanilla Chocolate Chip biscuits — 80
- Vanilla Walnuts Tart — 81
- Blackberry Pie — 81
- Crispy Bananas — 82
- Peach, Plum, and Nectarine Skewers — 82
- Baked Blueberries and Peaches — 83
- Peach and Apple Crumble — 83

Appendix 1 Measurement Conversion Chart — 84
Appendix 2 The Dirty Dozen and Clean Fifteen — 85
Appendix 3 Index — 86

Introduction

A UK Tower Air Fryer is a convenient appliance for cooking all types of food. It cuts cooking time, improves taste, and reduces oil to ensure healthy meals. For most people, there is the mistaken assumption that you can only cook French fries with it. A whole world of culinary delights will be unlocked with the Tower Air Fryer.

Most recipes for which you need an air fryer are 30 minutes or less. You can make a light breakfast, a full lunch, or even dinner for a small family. Many people love their air fryers so much that they get a second one to cook more. Everything from chicken to fish, roasted vegetables, and desserts can be prepared in an air fryer.

Chapter 1
Basics of Tower Air Fryer

What is An Air Fryer?

Many have heard of the air fryer, but a select few still have one. One reason is that they may need help understanding what it is and why they need it. An air fryer is a compact countertop oven that allows you to enjoy fried delights with all the unhealthy oil. With an air fryer, you can bake and roast food with a button.

Food made in an air fryer mimics the frying process while leaving out all the oil needed. It cooks food in half the time it would take a conventional oven. To cook food, it circulates superheated air into a basket holding the food, which browns and crisps it. Today, air fryers come in different sizes to accommodate different needs.

MEALS TO COOK IN A TOWER AIR FRYER?
Cooking using an air fryer is a quick, simple process that requires minimal effort. Most meals can be prepared in 30 minutes or less. The recipes require minimal preparation, and the cooking process is hands-off.

You can prepare foods ahead of cooking and store them in the fridge or freezer for later cooking. Best of all, air fryer recipes use simple ingredients that anyone can access in their local store. As a result, you get budget-friendly meals with the quality, flavor, and taste of a top-tier restaurant. The recipes below have been carefully crafted to take you on a culinary journey. You will love them for their simplicity and ease of preparation.

Besides fried chicken and chips, you can do a lot more with the air fryer. It can cook almost anything in an oven or deep fryer. Veggies cook great in an air fryer and come out light and crispy. Meat and fish cook well, with some models having two compartments that let you cook fish and veggies at once.

Some advanced Tower air fryers even have a rotisserie function, allowing you to cook a whole rotisserie chicken there. In some air fryers, you can even prepare stir-fries and curries. Some newer models even have a dehydration mode, which allows you to dehydrate fruit to enjoy delicious snacks and tasty breakfast toppings.

Air Fryers Are An Upgrade on Deep Fryers

Kitchen counter space is limited for most people. With so many appliances to pick from for specialized purposes, it can quickly clutter even a large countertop. An air fryer helps you eliminate the clutter for one convenient device.

An air fryer has been compared to an oven since it bakes and roasts. However, there is a massive difference in how it serves its purpose. Air fryers use a powerful fan at the top to blast food with superheated air. It ensures that food is evenly cooked with less oil than deep fryers. Another benefit of using the air fryer is the cleanup process. The Tower Air Fryer uses a basket and rack that is dishwasher-safe. After every meal, cleaning it will take you only a few seconds.

Deep fryers are good at cooking food. However, they require a giant vat of oil, heated to a set temperature, to cook the food. Because of the use of oil, you can cook only a limited selection of meals with a deep fryer. For instance, it is impossible to deep fry vegetables and have them taste good.

Another issue with a deep fryer is that it needs to be preheated. With an air fryer, you stick the food in there, and it immediately starts blasting it with hot air. Food comes out crispy and juicy. However, with an air fryer, the food tastes different. With a deep fryer, the taste of the oil can be overwhelming. The only downside with an air fryer is that it is difficult to cook foods covered in wet batter.

ENJOY HEALTHY MEALS

One of the main benefits of using an air fryer is how much less oil you need. In some preparations, you do not need any oil at all. In general, using an air fryer is healthier than deep-frying. If you are committed to using oil, you only need one teaspoon of oil in the air fryer. Health experts agree that any appliance that lets you enjoy tasty veggies easily is good for you. They also agree that any meal with less oil than a deep-fried meal is the best for your health.

Cleaning the Air Fryer

The basics of cleaning an air fryer are simple. First, it has to be unplugged from the power. Once it has cooled, wash the basket and handle in soapy water. For the inner parts, use a soft, damp cloth.

A brush can be used to clean tight spaces if some food has splattered on the heating element. If you do not clean it often, oil can build up, making it sticky and hard to clean. Each air fryer model is unique. To get the best results when cleaning, use the convenient manual that comes with it.

GREAT MEALS AT A LOW COST

One significant upside to getting an air fryer is how cheap it is. With the appliance being so popular, the price has come down significantly. Many models today come at less than $100. Get your Tower Air Fryer and enjoy the healthy recipes detailed below!

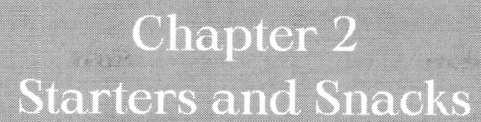

Chapter 2
Starters and Snacks

Ham and Cheese Stuffed Peppers

Prep time: 5 minutes | Cook time: 7 minutes | Serves 4

- 8 Serrano peppers
- 4 ounces (113 g) ham cubes
- 4 ounces (113 g) goat cheese, crumbled

1. Start by preheating the air fryer to 190°C.
2. Stuff the peppers with ham and cheese; transfer them to a lightly oiled crisper tray.
3. Place the crisper tray in the corresponding position in the air fryer. Select Air Fry and cook the peppers for about 7 minutes or until golden brown.
4. Bon appétit!

Coriander and Onion Pakoras

Prep time: 5 minutes | Cook time: 10 minutes per batch | Serves 2

- ½ cup chopped fresh Coriander
- 2 medium yellow onions, sliced (2 cups)
- 1 tablespoon chickpea flour
- 1 tablespoon ground rice
- 1 teaspoon ground turmeric
- 1 teaspoon cumin seeds
- 2 tablespoons vegetable oil
- 1 teaspoon flaked salt
- ½ teaspoon cayenne pepper
- Cooking spray

1. In a large bowl, combine the Coriander, onions, chickpea flour, ground rice, turmeric, cumin seeds, oil, salt, and cayenne. Stir to combine. Cover and let stand for 30 minutes or up to overnight.
2. Preheat the air fryer to 180°C. Spritz the air fryer basket or wire rack with cooking spray.
3. Drop half of the batter in 6 heaping tablespoons into the air fryer basket or wire rack. Air fry for 8 minutes. Carefully turn the pakoras over and air fry for 2 more minutes, or until the batter is cooked through and crisp.
4. Repeat with remaining batter to make 6 more pakoras. Serve hot.

Italian Rice Balls

Prep time: 20 minutes | Cook time: 10 minutes | Makes 8 rice balls

- 1½ cups cooked sticky rice
- ½ teaspoon Italian seasoning blend
- ¾ teaspoon salt, divided
- 8 black olives, pitted
- 1 ounce (28 g) Mozzarella cheese, cut into tiny pieces (small enough to stuff into olives)
- 2 eggs
- ⅓ cup Italian bread crumbs
- ¾ cup panko bread crumbs
- Cooking spray

1. Stuff each black olive with a piece of Mozzarella cheese.
2. In a bowl, combine the cooked sticky rice, Italian seasoning blend, and ½ teaspoon of salt and stir to mix well. Form the rice mixture into a log with your hands and divide it into 8 equal portions. Mold each portion around a black olive and roll into a ball.
3. Transfer to the freezer to chill for 10 to 15 minutes until firm.
4. In a shallow dish, place the Italian bread crumbs. In a separate shallow dish, whisk the eggs. In a third shallow dish, combine the panko bread crumbs and remaining salt.
5. One by one, roll the rice balls in the Italian bread crumbs, then dip in the whisked eggs, finally coat them with the panko bread crumbs.
6. Arrange the rice balls in the air fry basket and spritz both sides with cooking spray.
7. Select Air Fry, set temperature to 200°C, and set time to 10 minutes. Select Start/Stop to begin preheating.
8. Once preheated, place the air fryer basket or wire rack on the air fry position. Flip the balls halfway through the cooking time.
9. When cooking is complete, the rice balls should be golden brown. Remove from the oven and serve warm.

Panko-Crusted Artichoke Bites

Prep time: 5 minutes | Cook time: 8 minutes | Serves 4

- 14 whole artichoke hearts packed in water
- ½ cup plain flour
- 1 egg
- ⅓ cup panko bread crumbs
- 1 teaspoon Italian seasoning
- Cooking spray

1. Drain the artichoke hearts and dry thoroughly with kitchen paper.
2. Place the flour on a plate. Beat the egg in a shallow bowl until frothy. Thoroughly combine the bread crumbs and Italian seasoning in a separate shallow bowl.
3. Dredge the artichoke hearts in the flour, then in the beaten egg, and finally roll in the bread crumb mixture until evenly coated.
4. Place the artichoke hearts in the air fry basket and mist them with cooking spray.
5. Select Air Fry, set temperature to 190°C, and set time to 8 minutes. Select Start/Stop to begin preheating.
6. Once preheated, place the air fryer basket or wire rack on the air fry position. Flip the artichoke hearts halfway through the cooking time.
7. When cooking is complete, the artichoke hearts should start to brown and the edges should be crispy. Remove the air fryer basket or wire rack from the oven. Let the artichoke hearts sit for 5 minutes before serving.

Wax Beans with Cumin

Prep time: 6 minutes | Cook time: 6 minutes | Serves 4

- 1 pound (454 g) fresh wax beans, trimmed
- 2 teaspoons olive oil
- ½ teaspoon onion powder
- 1 teaspoon garlic powder
- ½ teaspoon cumin powder
- Sea salt and ground black pepper, to taste

1. Start by preheating the air fryer to 200°C.
2. Toss the wax beans with the remaining ingredients. Transfer to the crisper tray.
3. Place the crisper tray in the corresponding position in the air fryer. Select Air Fry and cook the wax beans for about 6 minutes, tossing the crisper tray halfway through the cooking time.
4. Enjoy!

Spicy Corn Tortilla Chips

Prep time: 5 minutes | Cook time: 5 minutes | Serves 4

- ½ teaspoon ground cumin
- ½ teaspoon paprika
- ½ teaspoon chili powder
- ½ teaspoon salt
- Pinch cayenne pepper
- 8 (6-inch) corn tortillas, each cut into 6 wedges
- Cooking spray

1. Lightly spritz the air fry basket with cooking spray.
2. Stir together the cumin, paprika, chili powder, salt, and pepper in a small bowl.
3. Place the tortilla wedges in the air fry basket in a single layer. Lightly mist them with cooking spray. Sprinkle the seasoning mixture on top of the tortilla wedges.
4. Select Air Fry, set temperature to 190°C, and set time to 5 minutes. Select Start/Stop to begin preheating.
5. Once preheated, place the air fryer basket or wire rack on the air fry position. Stir the tortilla wedges halfway through the cooking time.
6. When cooking is complete, the chips should be lightly browned and crunchy. Remove the air fryer basket or wire rack from the oven. Let the tortilla chips cool for 5 minutes and serve.

Turkey Bacon-Wrapped Dates

Prep time: 10 minutes | Cook time: 6 minutes | Makes 16 Starters

- 16 whole dates, pitted
- 16 whole almonds
- 6 to 8 strips turkey bacon, cut in half

SPECIAL EQUIPMENT:
- 16 Cocktail Sticks, soaked in water for at least 30 minutes

1. On a flat work surface, stuff each pitted date with a whole almond.
2. Wrap half slice of bacon around each date and secure it with a toothpick.
3. Place the bacon-wrapped dates in the air fry basket.
4. Select Air Fry, set temperature to 200°C, and set time to 6 minutes. Select Start/Stop to begin preheating.
5. Once preheated, place the air fryer basket or wire rack on the air fry position.
6. When cooking is complete, transfer the dates to a paper towel-lined plate to drain. Serve hot.

Aubergine with Paprika

Prep time: 5 minutes | Cook time: 15 minutes | Serves 3

- ¾ pound (340 g) aubergine
- Sea salt and ground black pepper, to taste
- ½ teaspoon paprika
- 2 tablespoons olive oil
- 2 tablespoons balsamic vinegar

1. Start by preheating the air fryer to 200°C.
2. Toss the aubergine pieces with the remaining ingredients until they are well coated on all sides.
3. Arrange the aubergine in the crisper tray.
4. Place the crisper tray in the corresponding position in the air fryer. Select Air Fry and cook the aubergine for about 15 minutes, shaking the crisper tray halfway through the cooking time.
5. Bon appétit!

Olive Nuggets

Prep time: 20 minutes | Cook time: 15 minutes | Serves 24 to 26 nuggets

- 1 (7-ounce / 198-g) jar pimento-stuffed green olives
- 1 cup Monterey Jack & Cheddar-style shreds
- 1 cup self-raising flour
- 1½ tablespoons all-vegetable shortening
- 3 tablespoons almond milk
- Oil for misting
- Strawberry jam (optional)

1. Drain the olives and blot them dry on kitchen paper.
2. Chop the cheese shreds and place them in a medium bowl.
3. Add the flour to the cheese shreds and mix together with your hands.
4. Still using your hands, work the shortening into the mixture until it's well blended.
5. Work in the milk until a dough forms.
6. Using 1½ teaspoons of dough for each olive, roll the dough into a ball, then flatten the ball into a disc about 2½ inches in diameter.
7. Lay the olive in the center of the dough and wrap the dough around the olive, squeezing and pinching to seal it.
8. Repeat to make 12 or 13 nuggets.
9. Mist the nuggets with oil and place them in the air fryer basket or wire rack in a single layer.
10. Cook at 200°C for 13 to 15 minutes, until they brown.
11. Repeat steps 6 through 10 to cook the remaining nuggets.
12. Serve with Strawberry Jam for dipping if you like.

Cheese Stuffed Mushrooms

Prep time: 10 minutes | Cook time: 7 minutes | Serves 4

- 1 tablespoon butter
- 6 ounces (170 g) Pecorino Romano cheese, grated
- 2 tablespoons chopped chives
- 1 tablespoon minced garlic
- ½ teaspoon cayenne pepper
- Sea salt and ground black pepper, to taste
- 1 pound (454 g) button mushrooms, stems removed

1. Start by preheating the air fryer to 200°C.
2. In a mixing bowl, thoroughly combine the butter, cheese, chives, garlic, cayenne pepper, salt, and black pepper.
3. Divide the filling between the mushrooms. Arrange the mushrooms in the crisper tray.
4. Place the crisper tray in the corresponding position in the air fryer. Select Air Fry and cook the mushrooms for about 7 minutes, shaking the crisper tray halfway through the cooking time.
5. Bon appétit!

Veggie Prawn Toast

Prep time: 15 minutes | **Cook time:** 6 minutes | **Serves 4**

- 8 large raw Prawn, peeled and finely chopped
- 1 egg white
- 2 garlic cloves, minced
- 3 tablespoons minced red bell pepper
- 1 medium celery stalk, minced
- 2 tablespoons cornflour
- ¼ teaspoon Chinese five-spice powder
- 3 slices firm thin-sliced no-sodium whole-wheat bread

1. Preheat the air fryer oven to 180°C.
2. In a small bowl, stir together the Prawn, egg white, garlic, red bell pepper, celery, cornflour, and five-spice powder. Top each slice of bread with one-third of the Prawn mixture, spreading it evenly to the edges. With a sharp knife, cut each slice of bread into 4 strips.
3. Place the Prawn toasts in the air fryer basket or wire rack in a single layer.
4. Place the air fryer basket or wire rack onto the baking pan, select Air Fry and set time to 6 minutes, or until crisp and golden brown.
5. Serve hot.

Breaded Green Tomatoes with Horseradish

Prep time: 15 minutes | **Cook time:** 13 minutes | **Serves 4**

- 2 eggs
- ¼ cup buttermilk
- ½ cup bread crumbs
- ½ cup cornmeal
- ¼ teaspoon salt
- 1½ pounds (680 g) firm green tomatoes, cut into ¼-inch slices
- Cooking spray
- Horseradish Sauce:
- ¼ cup Soured cream
- ¼ cup mayonnaise
- 2 teaspoons prepared horseradish
- ½ teaspoon lemon juice
- ½ teaspoon Worcestershire sauce
- ⅛ teaspoon black pepper

1. Spritz the air fry basket with cooking spray. Set aside.
2. In a small bowl, whisk together all the ingredients for the horseradish sauce until smooth. Set aside.
3. In a shallow dish, beat the eggs and buttermilk.
4. In a separate shallow dish, thoroughly combine the bread crumbs, cornmeal, and salt.
5. Dredge the tomato slices, one at a time, in the egg mixture, then roll in the bread crumb mixture until evenly coated.
6. Place the tomato slices in the air fry basket in a single layer. Spray them with cooking spray.
7. Select Air Fry, set temperature to 200°C, and set time to 13 minutes. Select Start/Stop to begin preheating.
8. Once preheated, place the air fryer basket or wire rack on the air fry position. Flip the tomato slices halfway through the cooking time.
9. When cooking is complete, the tomato slices should be nicely browned and crisp. Remove from the oven to a platter and serve drizzled with the prepared horseradish sauce.

Chile Pork Ribs

Prep time: 5 minutes | Cook time: 35 minutes | Serves 4

- 1½ pounds (680 g) spare ribs
- flake salt and ground black pepper, to taste
- 2 teaspoons Demerara sugar
- 1 teaspoon paprika
- 1 teaspoon chile powder
- 1 teaspoon garlic powder

1. Start by preheating the air fryer to 180°C.
2. Toss all the ingredients in a lightly greased crisper tray.
3. Place the crisper tray in the corresponding position in the air fryer. Select Air Fry and cook the pork ribs for 35 minutes, turning them over halfway through the cooking time.
4. Bon appétit!

Baked Sardines with Tomato Sauce

Prep time: 10 minutes | Cook time: 20 minutes | Serves 4

- 2 pounds (907 g) fresh Sardines
- 3 tablespoons olive oil, divided
- 4 Roma tomatoes, peeled and chopped
- 1 small onion, sliced thinly
- Zest of 1 orange
- Sea salt and freshly ground pepper, to taste
- 2 tablespoons whole-wheat bread crumbs
- ½ cup white wine

1. Brush a sheet pan with a little olive oil. Set aside.
2. Rinse the Sardines under running water. Slit the belly, remove the spine and butterfly the fish. Set aside.
3. Heat the remaining olive oil in a large frying pan. Add the tomatoes, onion, orange zest, salt and pepper to the frying pan and simmer for 20 minutes, or until the mixture thickens and softens.
4. Place half the sauce in the bottom of the sheet pan. Arrange the Sardines on top and spread the remaining half the sauce over the fish. Sprinkle with the bread crumbs and drizzle with the white wine.
5. Slide the pan into the air fryer. Press the Power Button. Cook at 200°C for 20 minutes.
6. When cooking is complete, remove from the air fryer. Serve immediately.

Broiled Prosciutto-Wrapped Pears

Prep time: 12 minutes | Cook time: 6 minutes | Serves 8

- 2 large, ripe Anjou pears
- 4 thin slices Parma prosciutto
- 2 teaspoons aged balsamic vinegar

1. Peel the pears. Slice into 8 wedges and cut out the core from each wedge.
2. Cut the prosciutto into 8 long strips. Wrap each pear wedge with a strip of prosciutto. Place the wrapped pears in a sheet pan.
3. Slide the pan into the air fryer. Cook for 6 minutes.
4. After 2 or 3 minutes, check the pears. The pears should be turned over if the prosciutto is beginning to crisp up and brown. Return to the air fryer and continue cooking.
5. When cooking is complete, remove from the air fryer. Drizzle the pears with the balsamic vinegar and serve warm.

Browned Ricotta with Capers and Lemon

Prep time: 10 minutes | Cook time: 8 minutes | Serves 4 to 6

- 1½ cups whole milk ricotta cheese
- 2 tablespoons extra-virgin olive oil
- 2 tablespoons capers, rinsed
- Zest of 1 lemon, plus more for garnish
- 1 teaspoon finely chopped fresh rosemary
- Pinch crushed red pepper flakes
- Salt and freshly ground black pepper, to taste
- 1 tablespoon grated Parmesan cheese

1. In a mixing bowl, stir together the ricotta cheese, olive oil, capers, lemon zest, rosemary, red pepper flakes, salt, and pepper until well combined.
2. Spread the mixture evenly in a baking dish.
3. Slide the baking dish into the air fryer. Press the Power Button. Cook at 190°C for 8 minutes.
4. When cooking is complete, the top should be nicely browned. Remove from the air fryer and top with a sprinkle of grated Parmesan cheese. Garnish with the lemon zest and serve warm.

Bruschetta with Tomato and Basil

Prep time: 5 minutes | Cook time: 3 minutes | Serves 6

- 4 tomatoes, diced
- ⅓ cup shredded fresh basil
- ¼ cup shredded Parmesan cheese
- 1 tablespoon balsamic vinegar
- 1 tablespoon minced garlic
- 1 teaspoon olive oil
- 1 teaspoon salt
- 1 teaspoon freshly ground black pepper
- 1 loaf French bread, cut into 1-inch-thick slices
- Cooking spray

1. Mix the tomatoes and basil in a medium bowl. Add the cheese, vinegar, garlic, olive oil, salt, and pepper and stir until well incorporated. Set aside.
2. Spritz the air flow racks with cooking spray and lay the bread slices in the racks. Spray the slices with cooking spray.
3. Slide the racks into the air fryer. Press the Power Button. Cook at 120°C for 3 minutes.
4. When cooking is complete, remove from the air fryer to a plate. Top each slice with a generous spoonful of the tomato mixture and serve.

Roasted Grapes with Yogurt

Prep time: 5 minutes | Cook time: 10 minutes | Serves 6

- 2 cups seedless red grapes, rinsed and patted dry
- 1 tablespoon apple cider vinegar
- 1 tablespoon honey
- 1 cup low-fat Greek yogurt
- 2 tablespoons 2 percent milk
- 2 tablespoons minced fresh basil

1. Spread the red grapes in the air flow racks and drizzle with the cider vinegar and honey. Lightly toss to coat.
2. Slide the racks into the air fryer. Press the Power Button. Cook at 190°C for 10 minutes.
3. When cooking is complete, the grapes will be wilted but still soft. Remove from the air fryer.
4. In a medium bowl, whisk together the yogurt and milk. Gently fold in the grapes and basil.
5. Serve immediately.

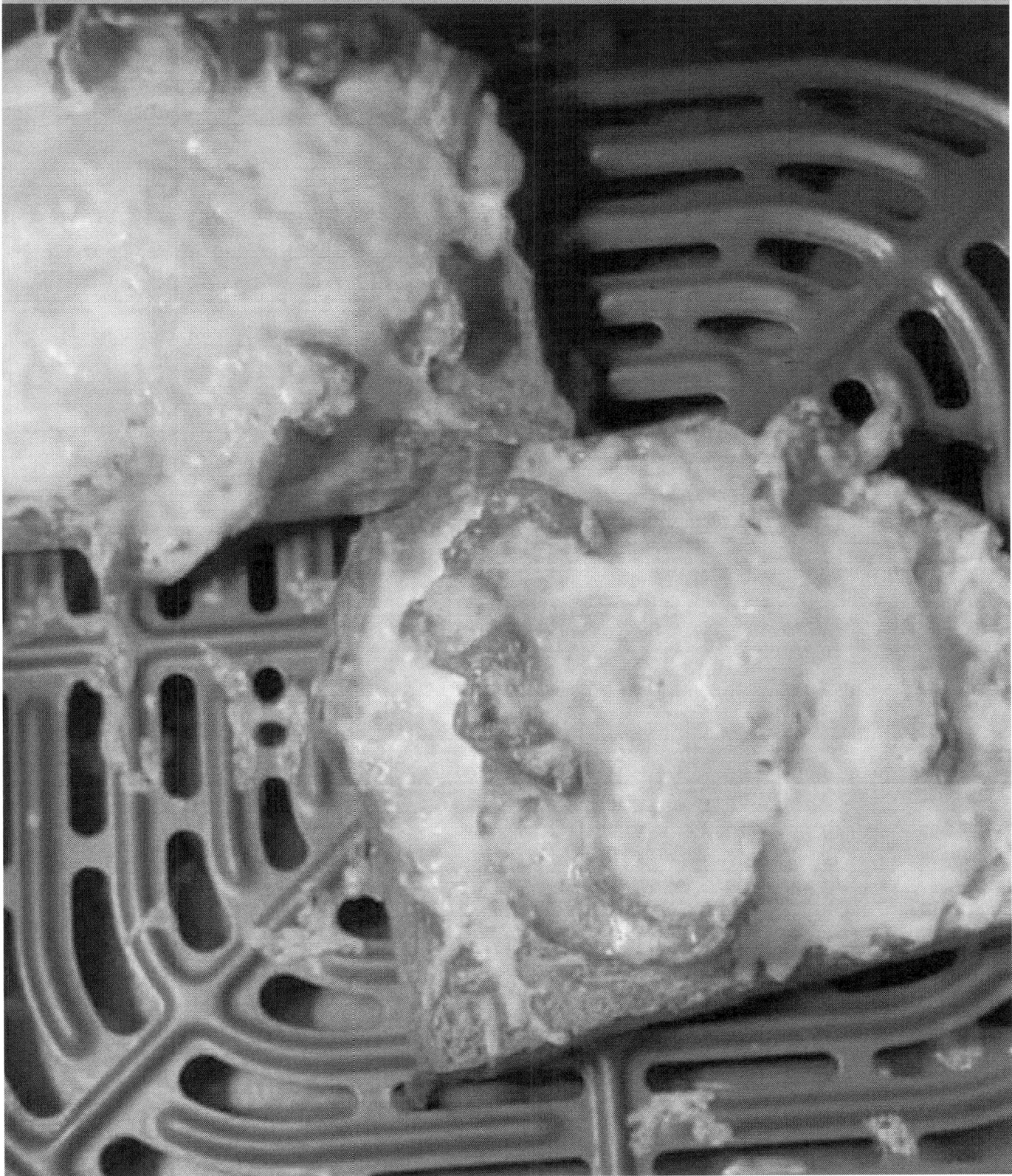

Chapter 3
Breakfast

Soft Pita Breads

Prep time: 10 minutes | **Cook time:** 6 minutes | **Serves** 8 mini pitas

- 2 teaspoons active dry yeast
- 1 tablespoon sugar
- 1¼ to 1½ cups warm water (90°F - 110°F)
- 3¼ cups plain flour
- 2 teaspoons salt
- 1 tablespoon olive oil, plus more for brushing
- flake salt(optional)

1. Dissolve the yeast, sugar and water in the bowl of a stand mixer. Let the mixture sit for 5 minutes to make sure the yeast is active – it should foam a little. (If there's no foaming, discard and start again with new yeast.) Combine the flour and salt in a bowl, and add it to the water, along with the olive oil. Mix with the dough hook until combined. Add a little more flour if needed to get the dough to pull away from the sides of the mixing bowl, or add a little more water if the dough seems too dry.
2. Knead the dough until it is smooth and elastic (about 8 minutes in the mixer or 15 minutes by hand). Transfer the dough to a lightly oiled bowl, cover and let it rise in a warm place until doubled in bulk.
3. Divide the dough into 8 portions and roll each portion into a circle about 4-inches in diameter. Don't roll the balls too thin, or you won't get the pocket inside the pita.
4. Pre-heat the air fryer to 200°C.
5. Brush both sides of the dough with olive oil, and sprinkle with flake saltif desired. Air-fry one at a time at 200°C for 6 minutes, flipping it over when there are two minutes left in the cooking time.

Tomato-Avocado Toast

Prep time: 5 minutes | **Cook time:** 0 minutes | **Serves** 2

- 2 slices thick whole grain bread
- 4 thin tomato slices
- 1 ripe avocado, pitted, peeled, and sliced
- 1 tablespoon olive oil
- 1 tablespoon pinch of salt
- ½ teaspoon chili flakes

1. Preheat air fryer to 190°C. Arrange the bread slices on the fryer and toast on Bake mode. Add the avocado to a bowl and mash it up with a fork until smooth. Season with salt.
2. When the toasted bread is ready, remove it to a plate. Drizzle with olive oil and arrange the thin tomato slices on top. Spread the avocado mash on top. Sprinkle the toasts with chili flakes and serve

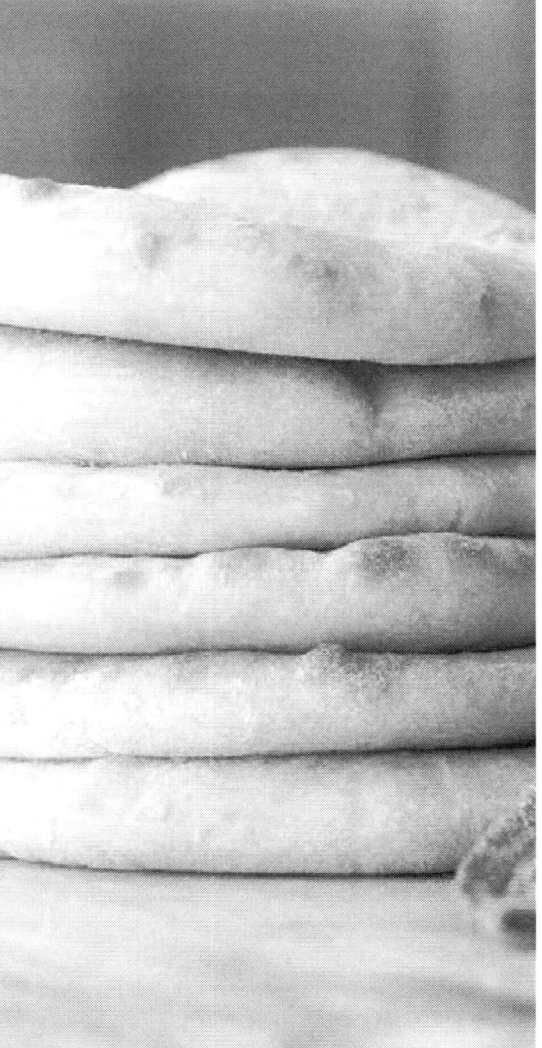

Turkey-Mushroom Burger

Prep time: 10 minutes | Cook time: 0 minutes | Serves 1

- ⅓ cup leftover turkey, shredded
- ⅓ cup sliced mushrooms, sauteed
- ½ tablespoon butter, softened
- 2 tomato slices
- ½ teaspoon red pepper flakes
- Salt and black pepper to taste
- 1 bap, halved

1. Preheat air fryer to 180°C. Brush the bottom half with butter and top with shredded turkey.
2. Arrange mushroom slices on top of the turkey. Cover with tomato slices and sprinkle with salt, black pepper, and red flakes.
3. Top with the other bun half and Air Fry in the fryer for 5 to 8 minutes until crispy.

Vegan Sandwich-Tofu with Cabbage

Prep time: 5 minutes | Cook time: 8 minutes | Serves 1

- 2 slices of bread
- 1 slice tofu, 1-inch thick
- ¼ cup red cabbage, shredded
- 2 teaspoon olive oil
- ¼ teaspoon vinegar
- Salt and black pepper to taste

1. Preheat air fryer to 180°C. Add the bread slices to the air fryer basket or wire rack and toast for 3 minutes; set aside. Brush the tofu with some olive oil and place in the air fryer to Bake for 5 minutes on each side.
2. Mix the cabbage, remaining olive oil, and vinegar. Season with salt. Place the tofu on top of one bread slice, place the cabbage over, and top with the other bread slice. Serve with cream cheese-mustard dip.

Muffins with Pecans and Kiwi

Prep time: 10 minutes | Cook time: 15 minutes | Serves 4

- 1 cup flour
- 1 kiwi, mashed
- ¼ cup icing sugar
- 1 teaspoon milk
- 1 tablespoon pecans, chopped
- ½ teaspoon baking powder
- ¼ cup oats
- ¼ cup butter, room temperature

1. Preheat air fryer to 180°C. Place the sugar, pecans, kiwi, and butter in a bowl and mix well. In another bowl, mix the flour, baking powder, and oats and stir well. Combine the two mixtures and stir in the milk.
2. Pour the batter into a greased muffin tin that fits in the fryer and bake for 15 minutes. Remove to a wire rack and leave to cool for a few minutes before removing from the muffin tin. Enjoy!

Sweet Raisins Bread

Prep time: 15 minutes | Cook time: 25 minutes | Serves 4

- 8 bread slices, cubed
- ½ cup buttermilk
- ¼ cup honey
- 1 cup milk
- 2 eggs
- ½ teaspoon vanilla extract
- 2 tablespoon butter, softened
- ¼ cup sugar
- 4 tablespoon raisins
- 2 tablespoon chopped hazelnuts
- Ground cinnamon for garnish

1. Preheat air fryer to 180°C. Beat the eggs with buttermilk, honey, milk, vanilla, sugar, and butter in a bowl.
2. Stir in raisins and hazelnuts, then add in the bread cubes to soak, about 10 minutes. Transfer to a greased tin and bake the pudding in fryer for 25 minutes. Dust with ground cinnamon and serve.

Vanilla-flavour Cherry Scones

Prep time: 10 minutes | Cook time: 14 minutes | Serves 4

- 2 cups flour + some more
- ⅓ cup sugar
- 2 teaspoon baking powder
- ½ cup sliced almonds
- ¾ cup chopped cherries, dried
- ¼ cup cold butter, cut into cubes
- ½ cup milk
- 1 egg
- 1 teaspoon vanilla extract

1. Line the air fryer basket or wire rack with baking paper. Mix together flour, sugar, baking powder, sliced almonds, and dried cherries in a bowl. Rub the butter into the dry ingredients with hands to form a sandy, crumbly texture.
2. Whisk together egg, milk, and vanilla extract. Pour into the dry ingredients and stir to combine. Sprinkle a working board with flour, lay the dough onto the board, and give it a few kneads. Shape into a rectangle and cut into 9 squares.
3. Arrange the squares in the air fryer's basket and cook for 14 minutes at 200°C. Work in batches if needed. Serve immediately.

Easy Deep-Fry Potatoes

Prep time: 10 minutes | Cook time: 20 minutes | Serves 6

- 4 large potatoes, cubed
- 2 bell peppers, cut into 1-inch chunks
- ½ onion, diced
- 2 teaspoon olive oil
- 1 garlic clove, minced
- ½ teaspoon dried thyme
- ½ teaspoon cayenne pepper
- Salt to taste

1. Preheat air fryer to 200°C. Place the potato cubes in a bowl and sprinkle with garlic, cayenne pepper, and salt. Drizzle with some olive oil and toss to coat.
2. Arrange the potatoes on an even layer on the greased air fryer basket or wire rack. Air Fry for 10 minutes, shaking the air fryer basket or wire rack once during the cooking time. In the meantime, add the remaining olive oil, garlic, thyme, and salt in a mixing bowl.
3. Add in the bell peppers and onion and mix well. Pour the veggies over the potatoes and continue cooking in the air fryer for 5 minutes.
4. At the 5-minute mark, shake the air fryer basket or wire rack and cook for 5 minutes. Serve warm.

Buttered Eggs in Bread Hole

Prep time: 5 minutes | Cook time: 8 minutes | Serves 2

- 2 bread slices
- 2 eggs
- Salt and black pepper to taste
- 2 tablespoon butter

1. Preheat air fryer to 180°C . Place a heatproof bowl in the fryer's basket and brush with butter.
2. Make a hole in the middle of the bread slices with a bread knife and place on the heatproof bowl in 2 batches.
3. Crack an egg into the center of each hole; season. Bake in the air fryer for 4 minutes.
4. Turn the bread with a spatula and cook for another 4 minutes. Serve warm.

Egg Pepper Rings with Cherry Tomatoes

Prep time: 5 minutes | Cook time: 9 minutes | Serves 4

- 4 eggs
- 1 bell pepper, cut into four ¾-inch rings
- 5 cherry tomatoes, halved
- Salt and black pepper to taste

1. Preheat air fryer to 180°C . Put the bell pepper rings in a greased baking pan and crack an egg into each one. Season with salt and pepper.
2. Top with the halved cherry tomatoes. Put the pan into the air fryer and air fry for 6 to 9 minutes, or until the eggs are have set. Serve and enjoy!

Parmesan Ranch Onion Risotto

Prep time: 10 minutes | Cook time: 30 minutes | Serves 2

- 1 tablespoon olive oil
- 1 clove garlic, minced
- 1 tablespoon unsalted butter
- 1 onion, diced
- ¾ cup Arborio rice
- 2 cups chicken stock, boiling
- ½ cup Parmesan cheese, grated

1. Preheat the air fryer to 200°C.
2. Grease a round baking tin with olive oil and stir in the garlic, butter, and onion.
3. Transfer the tin to the air fryer and bake for 4 minutes. Add the rice and bake for 4 more minutes.
4. Turn the air fryer to 160°C and pour in the chicken stock. Cover and bake for 22 minutes.
5. Scatter with cheese and serve.

Parmesan Egg and banger Muffins

Prep time: 5 minutes | Cook time: 20 minutes | Serves 4

- 6 ounces (170 g) Italian banger, sliced
- 6 eggs
- ⅛ cup double cream
- Salt and ground black pepper, to taste
- 3 ounces (85 g) Parmesan cheese, grated

1. Preheat the air fryer to 180°C. Grease a muffin pan.
2. Put the sliced banger in the muffin pan.
3. Beat the eggs with the cream in a bowl and season with salt and pepper.
4. Pour half of the mixture over the bangers in the pan.
5. Sprinkle with cheese and the remaining egg mixture.
6. Bake in the preheated air fryer for 20 minutes or until set.
7. Serve immediately.

Mozzarella Pepperoni Pizza

Prep time: 10 minutes | Cook time: 6 minutes | Serves 1

- 1 teaspoon olive oil
- 1 tablespoon pizza sauce
- 1 pita bread
- 6 pepperoni slices
- ¼ cup grated Mozzarella cheese
- ¼ teaspoon garlic powder
- ¼ teaspoon dried oregano

1. Preheat the air fryer to 180°C. Grease the baking pan with olive oil.
2. Spread the pizza sauce on top of the pita bread. Put the pepperoni slices over the sauce, followed by the Mozzarella cheese.
3. Season with garlic powder and oregano.
4. Put the pita pizza inside the air fryer and place a trivet on top.
5. Bake in the preheated air fryer for 6 minutes and serve.

Blueberry Muffins

Prep time: 10 minutes | Cook time: 12 minutes | Makes 8 muffins

- 1⅓ cups flour
- ½ cup sugar
- 2 teaspoons baking powder
- ¼ teaspoon salt
- ⅓ cup rapeseed oil
- 1 egg
- ½ cup milk
- ⅔ cup blueberries, fresh or frozen and thawed

1. Preheat the air fryer to 170°C.
2. In a medium bowl, stir together flour, sugar, baking powder, and salt.
3. In a separate bowl, combine oil, egg, and milk and mix well.
4. Add egg mixture to dry ingredients and stir just until moistened.
5. Gently stir in the blueberries.
6. Spoon batter evenly into greaseproof paper-lined muffin cups.
7. Put 4 muffin cups in the baking pan and bake for 12 minutes or until tops spring back when touched lightly.
8. Repeat previous step to bake remaining muffins.
9. Serve immediately.

Brown Rice Porridge with Coconut and Dates

Prep time: 5 minutes | Cook time: 23 minutes | Serves 1 or 2

- ½ cup cooked brown rice
- 1 cup tinned coconut milk
- ¼ cup unsweetened desiccated coconut
- ¼ cup packed dark Demerara sugar
- 4 large Medjool dates, pitted and roughly chopped
- ½ teaspoon flaked salt
- ¼ teaspoon ground cardamom
- double cream, for serving (optional)

1. Preheat the air fryer to 190°C.
2. Place all the ingredients except the double cream in a baking pan and stir until blended.
3. Transfer the pan to the air fryer and bake for about 23 minutes until the porridge is thick and creamy. Stir the porridge halfway through the cooking time.
4. Remove from the air fryer and ladle the porridge into bowls.
5. Serve hot with a drizzle of the cream, if desired.

Chapter 4
Poultry

Gai Yang Chicken

Prep time: 15 minutes | Cook time: 65 minutes | Serves 4

- 2-pounds Cornish hens, roughly chopped
- 2 tablespoons Gai yang spices
- 1 tablespoon avocado oil

1. Rub the hens with spices carefully.
2. Then sprinkle the hens with avocado oil and put in the air fryer.
3. Cook the meal at 180°C for 65 minutes.

Smoked Paprika Chicken

Prep time: 10 minutes | Cook time: 20 minutes | Serves 4

- 2-pounds chicken breast, skinless, boneless
- 1 tablespoon smoked paprika
- 1 teaspoon coconut oil, melted
- 1 tablespoon apple cider vinegar

1. In the shallow bowl, mix coconut oil with apple cider vinegar, and smoked paprika.
2. Carefully brush the chicken breast with smoked paprika mixture.
3. Then put the chicken in the air fryer and cook it at 190°C for 20 minutes. Flip the chicken on another side after 10 minutes of cooking.

Almond Meatballs

Prep time: 10 minutes | Cook time: 12 minutes | Serves 6

- 16 oz ground chicken
- ½ cup almond flour
- 1 teaspoon salt
- 1 teaspoon ground black pepper
- 1 tablespoon avocado oil

1. Mix ground chicken with almond flour, salt, and ground black pepper.
2. After this, make the meatballs and put them in the air fryer in one layer.
3. Sprinkle the meatballs with avocado oil and cook at 180°C for 12 minutes.

Sweet Chicken Wings

Prep time: 10 minutes | Cook time: 16 minutes | Serves 4

1-pound chicken wings
1 tablespoon taco seasonings
1 tablespoon Erythritol
1 tablespoon coconut oil, melted

1. Mix chicken wings with taco seasonings, Erythritol, and coconut oil.
2. Put the chicken wings in the air fryer basket or wire rack and cook them at 190°C for 16 minutes.

Parmesan and Dill Chicken

Prep time: 15 minutes | Cook time: 20 minutes | Serves 6

- 18 oz chicken breast, skinless, boneless
- 5 oz scratchings
- 3 oz Parmesan, grated
- 3 eggs, beaten
- 1 teaspoon chili flakes
- 1 teaspoon ground paprika
- 2 tablespoons avocado oil
- 1 teaspoon Erythritol
- ¼ teaspoon onion powder
- 1 teaspoon cayenne pepper
- 1 chili pepper, minced
- ½ teaspoon dried dill

1. In the shallow bowl mix up chili flakes, ground paprika, Erythritol. Onion powder, and cayenne pepper.
2. Add dried dill and stir the mixture gently. Then rub the chicken breast in the spice mixture. Then rub the chicken with minced chili pepper. Dip the chicken breast in the beaten eggs.
3. After this, coat it in the Parmesan and dip in the eggs again. Then coat the chicken in the pork rinds and sprinkle with avocado oil.
4. Preheat the air fryer to 190°C. Put the chicken breast in the air fryer and cook it for 16 minutes.
5. Then flip the chicken breast on another side and cook it for 4 minutes more.

Ginger and Coconut Chicken

Prep time: 5 minutes | Cook time: 20 minutes | Serves 4

- 4 chicken breasts, skinless, boneless and halved
- 4 tablespoons coconut aminos
- 1 teaspoon olive oil
- 2 tablespoons stevia
- Salt and black pepper to the taste
- ¼ cup chicken stock
- 1 tablespoon ginger, grated

1. In a pan that fits the air fryer, combine the chicken with the ginger and all the ingredients and toss.
2. Put the pan in your air fryer and cook at 200°C for 20, shaking the fryer halfway. Divide between plates and serve with a side salad.

Lemon Chicken Thighs

Prep time: 5 minutes | Cook time: 30 minutes | Serves 4

- 8 chicken thighs, boneless, skinless
- 1 tablespoon lemon zest, grated
- 2 tablespoons lemon juice
- 1 teaspoon avocado oil
- 1 teaspoon salt

1. Rub the chicken thighs with lemon zest, lemon juice, avocado oil, and salt.
2. Put the chicken thighs in the air fryer basket or wire rack and cook at 180°C for 30 minutes.
3. Flip the chicken thighs on another side after 15 minutes of cooking.

Basil Chicken Wings

Prep time: 5 minutes | Cook time: 30 minutes | Serves 4

- 2 pounds of chicken wings
- 1 tablespoon dried basil
- 1 teaspoon salt
- 1 tablespoon avocado oil

1. Sprinkle the chicken wings with dried basil, salt, and avocado oil.
2. Put the chicken wings in the air fryer basket or wire rack and cook at 180°C for 30 minutes.

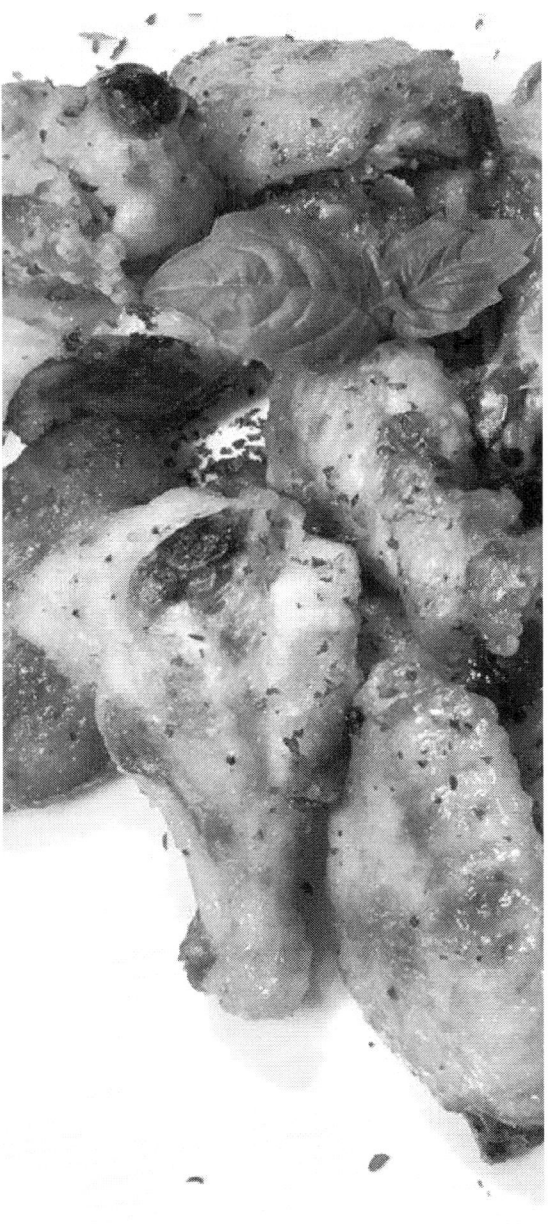

Lemon and Chili Chicken Drumsticks

Prep time: 10 minutes | Cook time: 20 minutes | Serves 6

- 6 chicken drumsticks
- 1 teaspoon dried oregano
- 1 tablespoon lemon juice
- ½ teaspoon lemon zest, grated
- 1 teaspoon ground cumin
- ½ teaspoon chili flakes
- 1 teaspoon garlic powder
- ½ teaspoon ground coriander
- 1 tablespoon avocado oil

1. Rub the chicken drumsticks with dried oregano, lemon juice, lemon zest, ground cumin, chili flakes, garlic powder, and ground coriander.
2. Then sprinkle them with avocado oil and put in the air fryer. Cook the chicken drumsticks for 20 minutes at 190°C.

BBQ Wings

Prep time: 10 minutes | Cook time: 20 minutes | Serves 4

- 2-pound chicken wings
- 1 cup BBQ sauce
- 1 teaspoon olive oil

1. Mix BBQ sauce with olive oil.
2. Brush the chicken wings carefully with the BQ sauce mixture and put it in the air fryer.
3. Cook the chicken wings for 9 minutes per side at 190°C.

Garlic Chicken Wings

Prep time: 5 minutes | Cook time: 30 minutes | Serves 4

- 2 pounds chicken wings
- ¼ cup olive oil
- Juice of 2 lemons
- Zest of 1 lemon, grated
- A pinch of salt and black pepper
- 2 garlic cloves, minced

1. In a bowl, mix the chicken wings with the rest of the ingredients and toss well.
2. Put the chicken wings in your air fryer's basket and cook at 400 degrees F for 30 minutes, shaking halfway.
3. Divide between plates and serve with a side salad.

Coriander Chicken Drumsticks

Prep time: 10 minutes | Cook time: 20 minutes | Serves 6

- 6 chicken drumsticks
- 1 tablespoon coconut oil, melted
- 1 tablespoon ground coriander
- 1 teaspoon garlic powder
- ½ teaspoon salt

1. Sprinkle the chicken drumsticks with ground coriander, salt, and garlic powder.
2. Then sprinkle the chicken drumsticks with coconut oil and put it in the air fryer.
3. Cook the meal at 190°C for 20 minutes.

Asparagus Chicken

Prep time: 15 minutes | Cook time: 30 minutes | Serves 4

- 1 cup asparagus, chopped
- 1-pound chicken thighs skinless, boneless
- 1 teaspoon onion powder
- 1 oz scallions, chopped
- 1 tablespoon coconut oil, melted
- 1 teaspoon smoked paprika

1. Mix chicken thighs with onion powder, coconut oil, and smoked paprika.
2. Put the chicken thighs in the air fryer and cook at 200°C for 20 minutes.
3. Then flip the chicken thighs on another side and top with chopped asparagus and scallions.
4. Cook the meal for 5 minutes more.

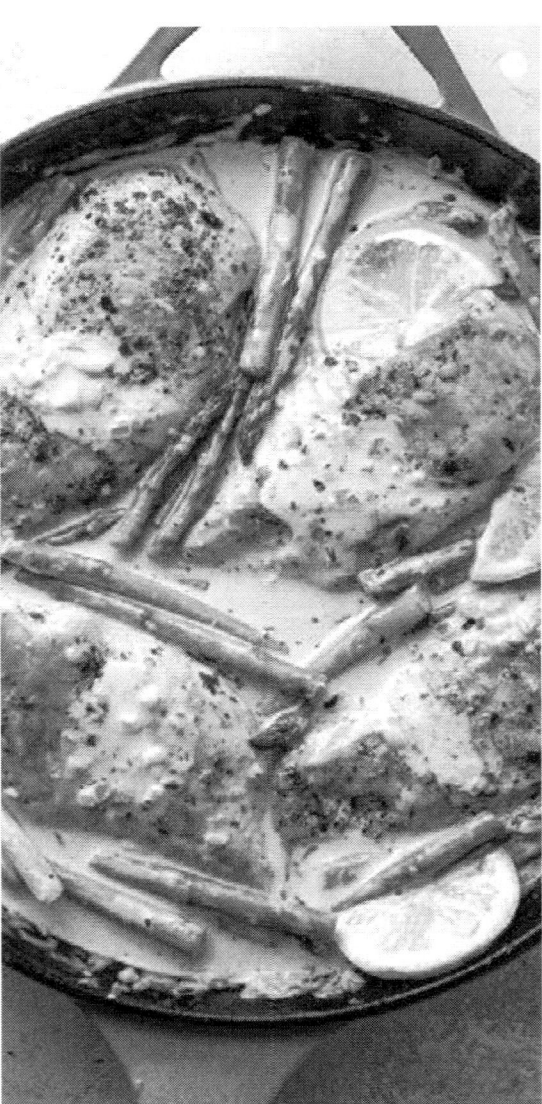

Nutmeg Chicken Fillets

Prep time: 15 minutes | Cook time: 12 minutes | Serves 4

- 16 oz chicken fillets
- 1 teaspoon ground nutmeg
- 1 tablespoon avocado oil
- ½ teaspoon salt

1. Mix ground nutmeg with avocado oil and salt.
2. Then rub the chicken fillet with a nutmeg mixture and put it in the air fryer basket or wire rack.
3. Cook the meal at 200°C for 12 minutes.

Chicken and Rice Casserole

Prep time: 5 minutes | Cook time: 35 minutes | Serves 4

- 2 cups cauliflower florets, chopped
- A pinch of salt and black pepper
- A drizzle of olive oil
- 6 ounces coconut cream
- 2 tablespoons butter, melted
- 2 teaspoons thyme, chopped
- 1 garlic clove, minced
- 1 tablespoon parsley, chopped
- 4 chicken thighs, boneless and skinless

1. Heat up a pan with the butter over medium heat, add the cream and the other ingredients except the cauliflower, oil and the chicken, whisk, bring to a simmer and cook for 5 minutes.
2. Heat up a pan with the oil over medium-high heat, add the chicken and brown for 2 minutes on each side.
3. In a baking dish that fits the air fryer, mix the chicken with the cauliflower, spread the coconut cream mix all over, put the pan in the machine and cook at 190°C for 20 minutes.
4. Divide between plates and serve hot.

Lemon Parmesan Chicken

Prep time: 10 minutes | Cook time: 20 minutes | Serves 4

- 1 egg
- 2 tablespoons lemon juice
- 2 teaspoons minced garlic
- ½ teaspoon salt
- ½ teaspoon freshly ground black pepper
- 4 boneless, skinless chicken breasts, thin cut
- Olive oil spray
- ½ cup whole-wheat bread crumbs
- ¼ cup grated Parmesan cheese

1. In a medium bowl, whisk together the egg, lemon juice, garlic, salt, and pepper. Add the chicken breasts, cover, and refrigerate for up to 1 hour.
2. In a shallow bowl, combine the bread crumbs and Parmesan cheese.
3. Spray the crisper tray lightly with olive oil spray.
4. Place the crisper tray on the air fry position. Select Air Fry, set the temperature to 180°C, and set the time to 20 minutes.
5. Remove the chicken breasts from the egg mixture, then dredge them in the bread crumb mixture, and place in the crisper tray in a single layer. Lightly spray the chicken breasts with olive oil spray. You may need to cook the chicken in batches.
6. Air fry for 8 minutes. Flip the chicken over, lightly spray with olive oil spray, and air fry for an additional 7 to 12 minutes, until the chicken reaches an internal temperature of 75°C.
7. Serve warm.

Lime Chicken Breasts with Coriander

Prep time: 35 minutes | Cook time: 10 minutes | Serves 4

- 4 (4-ounce / 113-g) boneless, skinless chicken breasts
- ½ cup chopped fresh Coriander
- Juice of 1 lime
- Chicken seasoning or rub, to taste
- Salt and ground black pepper, to taste
- Cooking spray

1. Put the chicken breasts in the large bowl, then add the Coriander, lime juice, chicken seasoning, salt, and black pepper. Toss to coat well.
2. Wrap the bowl in plastic and refrigerate to marinate for at least 30 minutes.
3. Spritz the perforated pan with cooking spray.
4. Remove the marinated chicken breasts from the bowl and place in the perforated pan. Spritz with cooking spray.
5. Select Air Fry. Set temperature to 200°C and set time to 10 minutes. Press Start to begin preheating.
6. Once preheated, place the pan into the oven. Flip the breasts halfway through.
7. When cooking is complete, the internal temperature of the chicken should reach at least 75°C.
8. Serve immediately.

Ground Chicken with Tomatoes

Prep time: 5 minutes | Cook time: 17 minutes | Serves 2

- 2 red bell peppers, chopped
- 1 pound (454 g) ground chicken
- 2 medium tomatoes, diced
- ½ cup chicken broth
- Salt and ground black pepper, to taste
- Cooking spray

1. Spritz a baking pan with cooking spray.
2. Set the bell pepper in the baking pan.
3. Select Broil. Set temperature to 180°C and set time to 5 minutes. Press Start to begin preheating.
4. Once preheated, place the pan into the oven. Stir the bell pepper halfway through.
5. When broiling is complete, the bell pepper should be tender.
6. Add the ground chicken and diced tomatoes in the baking pan and stir to mix well.
7. Set time to 12 minutes. Stir the mixture and mix in the chicken broth, salt and ground black pepper halfway through.
8. When cooking is complete, the chicken should be well browned.
9. Serve immediately.

Crispy Chicken Strips

Prep time: 15 minutes | Cook time: 20 minutes | Serves 4

- 1 tablespoon olive oil
- 1 pound (454 g) boneless, skinless chicken tenderloins
- 1 teaspoon salt
- ½ teaspoon freshly ground black pepper
- ½ teaspoon paprika
- ½ teaspoon garlic powder
- ½ cup whole-wheat seasoned bread crumbs
- 1 teaspoon dried parsley
- Cooking spray

1. Spray the crisper tray lightly with cooking spray.
2. Place the crisper tray on the air fry position. Select Air Fry, set the temperature to 190°C, and set the time to 20 minutes.
3. In a medium bowl, toss the chicken with the salt, pepper, paprika, and garlic powder until evenly coated.
4. Add the olive oil and toss to coat the chicken evenly.
5. In a separate, shallow bowl, mix together the bread crumbs and parsley.
6. Coat each piece of chicken evenly in the bread crumb mixture.
7. Place the chicken in the crisper tray in a single layer and spray it lightly with cooking spray. You may need to cook them in batches.
8. Air fry for 10 minutes. Flip the chicken over, lightly spray it with cooking spray, and air fry for an additional 8 to 10 minutes, until golden brown. Serve.

Chicken with Veggie Couscous Salad

Prep time: 25 minutes | Cook time: 20 minutes | Serves 4

- 3 tablespoons plus 2 teaspoons Cranberry Juice
- ½ teaspoon ground cinnamon
- 1 teaspoon minced fresh thyme
- Salt and ground black pepper, to taste
- 2 (12-ounce / 340-g) bone-in split chicken breasts, trimmed
- ¼ cup chicken broth
- ¼ cup water
- ½ cup couscous
- 1 tablespoon minced fresh parsley
- 2 ounces (57 g) cherry tomatoes, quartered
- 1 scallion, white part minced, green part sliced thin on bias
- 1 tablespoon extra-virgin olive oil
- 1 ounce (28 g) feta cheese, crumbled
- Cooking spray

1. Spritz the perforated pan with cooking spray.
2. Combine 3 tablespoons of Cranberry Juice, cinnamon, thyme, and ⅛ teaspoon of salt in a small bowl. Stir to mix well. Set aside.
3. Place the chicken breasts in the perforated pan, skin side down, and spritz with cooking spray. Sprinkle with salt and ground black pepper.
4. Select Air Fry. Set temperature to 180°C and set time to 20 minutes. Press Start to begin preheating.
5. Once preheated, place the pan into the oven. Flip the chicken and brush with Cranberry Juice mixture halfway through.
6. Meanwhile, pour the broth and water in a pot and bring to a boil over medium-high heat. Add the couscous and sprinkle with salt. Cover and simmer for 7 minutes or until the liquid is almost absorbed.
7. Combine the remaining ingredients, except for the cheese, with cooked couscous in a large bowl. Toss to mix well. Scatter with the feta cheese.
8. When cooking is complete, remove the chicken from the oven and allow to cool for 10 minutes. Serve with vegetable and couscous salad.

Chapter 5
Beef lamb and Pork

Crusted Pork Chops

Prep Time: 8 minutes | Cooking Time: 15 minutes | Servings: 4

- 2 Pork chops
- 3 tbsp. Olive oil
- 1 tbsp. Chopped rosemary
- Salt and pepper to taste
- 1 tbsp. fennel

1. In a bowl, add in the pork chops with the salt, fennel, Oil, pepper and the rosemary
2. Stir and ensure the pork chops coat well
3. Arrange the chops to your Air fryer and Cook for 15 minutes at 200°C
4. Share the chops between plates and serve

Beef Burger

Prep time: 20 minutes | Cook time: 12 minutes | Serves 4

- 1¼ pounds (567g) lean minced beef
- 1 tablespoon coconut aminos
- 1 teaspoon Dijon mustard
- A few dashes of liquid smoke
- 1 teaspoon shallot powder
- 1 clove garlic, minced
- ½ teaspoon cumin powder
- ¼ cup scallions, minced
- ⅓ teaspoon sea salt flakes
- ⅓ teaspoon freshly cracked mixed peppercorns
- 1 teaspoon celery seeds
- 1 teaspoon parsley flakes

1. Mix all of the above ingredients in a bowl; knead until everything is well incorporated.
2. Shape the mixture into four patties. Next, make a shallow dip in the center of each patty to prevent them puffing up during air-frying.
3. Spritz the patties on all sides using a non-stick cooking spray. Cook approximately 12 minutes at 180°C.
4. Check for doneness – an instant read thermometer should read 70°C. Bon appétit!

Classic Roast Beef

Prep time: 20 minutes | **Cook time:** 45 minutes | **Serves 8**

- 2 pounds (907 g) roast beef, at room temperature
- 2 tablespoons extra-virgin olive oil
- 1 teaspoon sea salt flakes
- 1 teaspoon black pepper, preferably freshly ground
- 1 teaspoon smoked paprika
- A few dashes of liquid smoke
- 2 jalapeño peppers, thinly sliced

1. Start by preheating the Air fryer to 170°C.
2. Then, pat the roast dry using kitchen towels. Rub with extra-virgin olive oil and all seasonings along with liquid smoke.
3. Roast for 30 minutes in the preheated Air fryer; then, pause the machine and turn the roast over; roast for additional 15 minutes.
4. Check for doneness using a meat thermometer and serve sprinkled with sliced jalapeños. Bon appétit!

Roast Beef Steaks

Prep time: 20 minutes | **Cook time:** 20 minutes | **Serves 4**

- 2 tablespoons coconut aminos
- 3 heaping tablespoons fresh chives
- 2 tablespoons olive oil
- 3 tablespoons dry white wine
- 4 small-sized beef steaks
- 2 teaspoons smoked cayenne pepper
- ½ teaspoon dried basil
- ½ teaspoon dried rosemary
- 1 teaspoon freshly ground black pepper
- 1 teaspoon sea salt, or more to taste

1. Firstly, coat the steaks with the cayenne pepper, black pepper, salt, basil, and rosemary.
2. Drizzle the steaks with olive oil, white wine, and coconut aminos.
3. Finally, roast in a air fryer basket or wire rack for 20 minutes at 170°C. Serve garnished with fresh chives. Bon appétit!

Air Fried Flank Steak

Prep time: 5 minutes | Cook time: 8 to 10 minutes | Serves 6

- ½ cup avocado oil
- ¼ cup coconut aminos
- 1 shallot, minced
- 1 tablespoon minced garlic
- 2 tablespoons chopped fresh oregano, or 2 teaspoons dried
- 1½ teaspoons sea salt
- 1 teaspoon freshly ground black pepper
- ¼ teaspoon red pepper flakes
- 2 pounds (907 g) flank steak

1. In a blender, combine the avocado oil, coconut aminos, shallot, garlic, oregano, salt, black pepper, and red pepper flakes. Process until smooth.
2. Place the steak in a zip-top plastic bag or shallow dish with the marinade. Seal the bag or cover the dish and marinate in the refrigerator for at least 2 hours or overnight.
3. Remove the steak from the bag and discard the marinade.
4. Set the Air fryer to 200°C. Place the steak in the air fryer basket or wire rack (if needed, cut into sections and work in batches). Cook for 4 to 6 minutes, flip the steak, and cook for another 4 minutes or until the internal temperature reaches 50°C in the thickest part (or as desired).

Cheesy Flank Steak

Prep time: 10 minutes | Cook time: 14 minutes | Serves 6

- 1 pound (454 g) flank steak
- 1 tablespoon avocado oil
- ½ teaspoon sea salt
- ½ teaspoon garlic powder
- ¼ teaspoon freshly ground black pepper
- 2 ounces (57 g) goat cheese, crumbled
- 1 cup baby spinach, chopped

1. Place the steak in a large zip-top bag or between two pieces of Cling Film. Using a meat mallet or heavy-bottomed frying pan, pound the steak to an even ¼-inch thickness.
2. Brush both sides of the steak with the avocado oil.
3. Mix the salt, garlic powder, and pepper in a small dish. Sprinkle this mixture over both sides of the steak.
4. Sprinkle the goat cheese over top, and top that with the spinach.
5. Starting at one of the long sides, roll the steak up tightly. Tie the rolled steak with kitchen string at 3-inch intervals.
6. Set the Air fryer to 200°C. Place the steak roll-up in the air fryer basket or wire rack. Cook for 7 minutes. Flip the steak and cook for an additional 7 minutes, until an instant-read thermometer reads 50°C (adjust the cooking time for your desired doneness).

Beef with Leeks

Prep Time: 8 minutes | Cooking Time: 15 minutes | Servings: 4

- 1 tbsp. Olive Oil
- 1 lb. minced beef
- 2 tbsp. tomato purée
- 3 leeks, roughly chopped
- Salt and black pepper to taste
- 1 tbsp. Baby rocket
- 2 tbsp. tomato purée

1. In a pan, mix in the beef with leeks, pepper, salt, tomato purée, and Oil
2. Put the pan in the Air fryer and Cook for 15 minutes 380°F
3. Add the rocket and toss
4. Serve into bowls and stir

Beef banger with Tomato Bowl

Prep time: 35 minutes | Cook time: 20 minutes | Serves 4

- 4 bell peppers
- 2 tablespoons olive oil
- 2 medium-sized tomatoes, halved
- 4 spring onions
- 4 beef bangers
- 1 tablespoon mustard

1. Start by preheating your Air fryer to 200°C.
2. Add the bell peppers to the cooking basket. Drizzle 1 tablespoon of olive oil all over the bell peppers.
3. Cook for 5 minutes. Turn the temperature down to 180°C. Add the tomatoes and spring onions to the cooking basket and cook an additional 10 minutes.
4. Reserve your vegetables.
5. Then, add the bangers to the cooking basket. Drizzle with the remaining tablespoon of olive oil.
6. Cook in the preheated Air fryer at 190°C for 15 minutes, flipping them halfway through the cooking time.
7. Serve bangers with the air-fried vegetables and mustard; serve.

Cheese Steak with Lettuce

Prep time: 15 minutes | **Cook time:** 8 to 10 minutes | **Serves 4**

- 1 pound (454 g) flank steak
- 1 teaspoon garlic powder
- 1 teaspoon ground cumin
- ½ teaspoon sea salt
- ½ teaspoon freshly ground black pepper
- 5 ounces (142 g) shredded Cos lettuce
- ½ cup crumbled feta cheese
- ½ cup peeled and diced cucumber
- ⅓ cup sliced red onion
- ¼ cup seeded and diced tomato
- 2 tablespoons pitted and sliced black olives
- Tzatziki Sauce, for serving

1. Pat the steak dry with kitchen paper. In a small bowl, combine the garlic powder, cumin, salt, and pepper. Sprinkle this mixture all over the steak, and allow the steak to rest at room temperature for 45 minutes.
2. Preheat the Air fryer to 200°C. Place the steak in the air fryer basket or wire rack and cook for 4 minutes. Flip the steak and cook 4 to 6 minutes more, until an instant-read thermometer reads 50°C at the thickest point (or as desired). Remove the steak from the Air fryer and let it rest for 5 minutes.
3. Divide the romaine among plates. Top with the feta, cucumber, red onion, tomato, and olives.
4. Thinly slice the steak diagonally. Add the steak to the plates and drizzle with tzatziki sauce before serving.

Courgette Noodle with Beef Meatball

Prep time: 15 minutes | **Cook time:** 11 to 13 minutes | **Serves 6**

- 1 pound (454 g) minced beef
- 1½ teaspoons sea salt, plus more for seasoning
- 1 large egg, beaten
- 1 teaspoon gelatin
- ¾ cup Parmesan cheese
- 2 teaspoons minced garlic
- 1 teaspoon Italian seasoning
- Freshly ground black pepper, to taste
- Avocado oil spray
- Keto-friendly marinara sauce,, for serving
- 6 ounces (170 g) courgette noodles, made using a spiralizer or store-bought

1. Place the minced beef in a large bowl, and season with the salt.
2. Place the egg in a separate bowl and sprinkle with the gelatin. Allow to sit for 5 minutes.
3. Stir the gelatin mixture, then pour it over the minced beef. Add the Parmesan, garlic, and Italian seasoning. Season with salt and pepper.
4. Form the mixture into 1½-inch meatballs and place them on a plate; cover with Cling Film and refrigerate for at least 1 hour or overnight.
5. Spray the meatballs with oil. Set the Air fryer to 200°C and arrange the meatballs in a single layer in the air fryer basket or wire rack. Cook for 4 minutes. Flip the meatballs and spray them with more oil. Cook for 4 minutes more, until an instant-read thermometer reads 70°C. Transfer the meatballs to a plate and allow them to rest.
6. While the meatballs are resting, heat the marinara in a saucepan on the cooker over medium heat.
7. Place the courgette noodles in the Air fryer, and cook at 200°C for 3 to 5 minutes.
8. To serve, place the courgette noodles in serving bowls. Top with meatballs and warm marinara.

Ribs with Chimichurri Sauce

Prep time: 15 minutes | Cook time: 13 minutes | Serves 4

- 1 pound (454 g) boneless short ribs
- 1½ teaspoons sea salt, divided
- ½ teaspoon freshly ground black pepper, divided
- ½ cup fresh parsley leaves
- ½ cup fresh Coriander leaves
- 1 teaspoon minced garlic
- 1 tablespoon freshly squeezed lemon juice
- ½ teaspoon ground cumin
- ¼ teaspoon red pepper flakes
- 2 tablespoons extra-virgin olive oil
- Avocado oil spray

1. Pat the short ribs dry with kitchen paper. Sprinkle the ribs all over with 1 teaspoon salt and ¼ teaspoon black pepper. Let sit at room temperature for 45 minutes.
2. Meanwhile, place the parsley, Coriander, garlic, lemon juice, cumin, red pepper flakes, the remaining ½ teaspoon salt, and the remaining ¼ teaspoon black pepper in a blender or food processor. With the blender running, slowly drizzle in the olive oil. Blend for about 1 minute, until the mixture is smooth and well combined.
3. Set the Air fryer to 200°C. Spray both sides of the ribs with oil. Place in the air fryer basket or wire rack and cook for 8 minutes. Flip and cook for another 5 minutes, until an instant-read thermometer reads 52°C (or to your desired doneness).
4. Allow the meat to rest for 5 to 10 minutes, then slice. Serve warm with the chimichurri sauce.

Beef Paprika

Prep Time: 6 minutes | Cooking Time: 26 minutes | Servings: 4

- 3 tbsp. Sweet Paprika
- 1 tbsp. Worcestershire sauce
- Salt and black pepper
- ½ cup beef stock
- 1 tbsp. tomato purée
- 1 Roughly chopped red onion
- 1½ lbs. Beef fillets
- 2 tbsp. Olive Oil

1. In a bowl and combine the beef with all the ingredients, mix well
2. Arrange the mixture to a pan that suits your Air fryer and Cook for 26 minutes at 200°C
3. Serve between plates.

Breaded Pork Loin Chops

Prep time: 5 minutes | Cook time: 10 minutes | Serves 4

- ⅔ cup plain flour
- 2 large egg whites
- 1 cup panko bread crumbs
- 4 (4-ounce / 113-g) center-cut boneless pork loin chops (about ½ inch thick)
- Cooking spray

1. Pour the flour in a bowl. Whisk the egg whites in a separate bowl. Spread the bread crumbs on a large plate.
2. Dredge the pork loin chops in the flour first, press to coat well, then shake the excess off and dunk the chops in the eggs whites, and then roll the chops over the bread crumbs. Shake the excess off.
3. Arrange the pork chops in the perforated pan and spritz with cooking spray.
4. Select Air Fry. Set temperature to 190°C and set time to 10 minutes. Press Start to begin preheating.
5. Once preheated, place the pan into the Air Fryer.
6. After 5 minutes, remove the pan from the Air Fryer. Flip the pork chops. Return the pan to the Air Fryer and continue cooking.
7. When cooking is complete, the pork chops should be crunchy and lightly browned.
8. Serve immediately.

Pork and Veggie Kebabs

Prep time: 25 minutes | Cook time: 15 minutes | Serves 4

- 1 pound (454 g) pork tenderloin, cubed
- 1 teaspoon smoked paprika
- Salt and ground black pepper, to taste
- 1 green bell pepper, cut into chunks
- 1 courgette, cut into chunks
- 1 red onion, sliced
- 1 tablespoon oregano
- Cooking spray

SPECIAL EQUIPMENT:

- Small bamboo skewers, soaked in water for 20 minutes to keep them from burning while cooking

1. Spritz the perforated pan with cooking spray.
2. Add the pork to a bowl and season with the smoked paprika, salt and black pepper. Thread the seasoned pork cubes and vegetables alternately onto the soaked skewers. Arrange the skewers in the pan.
3. Select Air Fry. Set temperature to 180°C and set time to 15 minutes. Press Start to begin preheating.
4. Once preheated, place the pan into the Air Fryer.
5. After 7 minutes, remove the pan from the Air Fryer. Flip the pork skewers. Return the pan to the Air Fryer and continue cooking.
6. When cooking is complete, the pork should be browned and vegetables are tender.
7. Transfer the skewers to the serving dishes and sprinkle with oregano. Serve hot.

Pork and Pineapple Kebabs

Prep time: 10 minutes | Cook time: 12 minutes | Serves 4

- ¼ teaspoon flake salt or ⅛ teaspoon fine salt
- 1 medium pork tenderloin (about 1 pound / 454 g) cut into 1½-inch chunks
- 1 green bell pepper, seeded and cut into 1-inch pieces
- 1 red bell pepper, seeded and cut into 1-inch pieces
- 2 cups fresh pineapple chunks
- ¾ cup Teriyaki Sauce or store-bought variety, divided

SPECIAL EQUIPMENT:
- 12 (9- to 12-inch) wooden skewers, soaked in water for about 30 minutes

1. Sprinkle the pork cubes with the salt.
2. Thread the pork, bell peppers, and pineapple onto a skewer. Repeat until all skewers are complete. Brush the skewers generously with about half of the Teriyaki Sauce. Place them on the sheet pan.
3. Select Roast. Set temperature to 190°C and set time to 10 minutes. Press Start to begin preheating.
4. Once the unit has preheated, place the pan into the Air Fryer.
5. After about 5 minutes, remove the pan from the Air Fryer. Turn over the skewers and brush with the remaining half of Teriyaki Sauce. Transfer the pan back to the Air Fryer and continue cooking until the vegetables are tender and browned in places and the pork is browned and cooked through.
6. Remove the pan from the Air Fryer and serve.

Bacon-Wrapped Pork Hot Dogs

Prep time: 5 minutes | Cook time: 10 minutes | Serves 5

- 10 thin slices of bacon
- 5 pork hot dogs, halved
- 1 teaspoon cayenne pepper

SAUCE:
- ¼ cup mayonnaise
- 4 tablespoons low-carb ketchup
- 1 teaspoon rice vinegar
- 1 teaspoon chili powder

1. Arrange the slices of bacon on a clean work surface. One by one, place the halved hot dog on one end of each slice, season with cayenne pepper and wrap the hot dog with the bacon slices and secure with Cocktail Sticks as needed.
2. Place wrapped hot dogs in the perforated pan.
3. Select Air Fry. Set temperature to 200°C and set time to 10 minutes. Press Start to begin preheating.
4. Once preheated, place the pan into the Air Fryer. Flip the bacon-wrapped hot dogs halfway through.
5. When cooking is complete, the bacon should be crispy and browned.
6. Make the sauce: Stir all the ingredients for the sauce in a small bowl. Wrap the bowl in plastic and set in the refrigerator until ready to serve.
7. Transfer the hot dogs to a platter and serve hot with the sauce.

BBQ kielbasa banger

Prep time: 15 minutes | Cook time: 10 minutes | Serves 2 to 4

- ¾ pound (340 g) kielbasa banger, cut into ½-inch slices
- 1 (8-ounce / 227-g) can pineapple chunks in juice, drained
- 1 cup bell pepper chunks
- 1 tablespoon barbecue seasoning
- 1 tablespoon soy sauce
- Cooking spray

1. Spritz the perforated pan with cooking spray.
2. Combine all the ingredients in a large bowl. Toss to mix well.
3. Pour the banger mixture in the perforated pan.
4. Select Air Fry. Set temperature to 200°C and set time to 10 minutes. Press Start to begin preheating.
5. Once preheated, place the pan into the Air Fryer.
6. After 5 minutes, remove the pan from the Air Fryer. Stir the banger mixture. Return the pan to the Air Fryer and continue cooking.
7. When cooking is complete, the banger should be lightly browned and the bell pepper and pineapple should be soft.
8. Serve immediately.

Chapter 6
Fish and Seafood

Honey-Glazed Cod with Sesame Seeds

Prep time: 5 minutes | Cook time: 7 to 9 minutes | Makes 1 fillet

- 1 tablespoon reduced-sodium soy sauce
- 2 teaspoons honey
- Cooking spray
- 6 ounces (170 g) fresh cod fillet
- 1 teaspoon sesame seeds

1. Preheat the air fryer to 180°C.
2. In a small bowl, combine the soy sauce and honey.
3. Spray the baking pan with cooking spray, then place the cod in the pan, brush with the soy mixture, and sprinkle sesame seeds on top. Bake for 7 to 9 minutes or until opaque.
4. Remove the fish and allow to cool on a wire rack for 5 minutes before serving.

Almond-Lemon Crusted Fish

Prep time: 10 minutes | Cook time: 9 minutes | Serves 4

- ½ cup raw whole almonds
- 1 scallion, finely chopped
- Grated zest and juice of 1 lemon
- ½ tablespoon extra-virgin olive oil
- ¾ teaspoon flaked salt, divided
- Freshly ground black pepper, to taste
- 4 (6 ounces / 170 g each) skinless fish fillets
- Cooking spray
- 1 teaspoon Dijon mustard

1. In a food processor, pulse the almonds to coarsely chop. Transfer to a small bowl and add the scallion, lemon zest, and olive oil. Season with ¼ teaspoon of the salt and pepper to taste and mix to combine.
2. Spray the top of the fish with oil and squeeze the lemon juice over the fish. Season with the remaining ½ teaspoon salt and pepper to taste. Spread the mustard on top of the fish. Dividing evenly, press the almond mixture onto the top of the fillets to adhere.
3. Preheat the air fryer to 200°C.
4. Working in batches, place the fillets in the baking pan in a single layer. Bake for 9 minutes, until the crumbs start to brown and the fish is cooked through.
5. Serve immediately.

Almond-Coconut Flounder Fillets

Prep time: 8 minutes | Cook time: 12 minutes | Serves 2

- 2 flounder fillets, patted dry
- 1 egg
- ½ teaspoon Worcestershire sauce
- ¼ cup almond flour
- ¼ cup coconut flour
- ½ teaspoon coarse sea salt
- ½ teaspoon lemon pepper
- ¼ teaspoon chili powder
- Cooking spray

1. Preheat the air fryer to 200°C. Spritz the baking pan with cooking spray.
2. In a shallow bowl, beat together the egg with Worcestershire sauce until well incorporated.
3. In another bowl, thoroughly combine the almond flour, coconut flour, sea salt, lemon pepper, and chili powder.
4. Dredge the fillets in the egg mixture, shaking off any excess, then roll in the flour mixture to coat well.
5. Place the fillets in the pan and bake for 7 minutes. Flip the fillets and spray with cooking spray. Continue cooking for 5 minutes, or until the fish is flaky.
6. Serve warm.

Lemon-Caper Salmon Burgers

Prep time: 15 minutes | Cook time: 15 minutes | Serves 5

- Lemon-Caper Rémoulade:
- ½ cup mayonnaise
- 2 tablespoons minced drained capers
- 2 tablespoons chopped fresh parsley
- 2 teaspoons fresh lemon juice

SALMON PATTIES:

- 1 pound (454 g) wild salmon fillet, skinned and pin bones removed
- 6 tablespoons panko bread crumbs
- ¼ cup minced red onion plus ¼ cup slivered for serving
- 1 garlic clove, minced
- 1 large egg, lightly beaten
- 1 tablespoon Dijon mustard
- 1 teaspoon fresh lemon juice
- 1 tablespoon chopped fresh parsley
- ½ teaspoon flaked salt

FOR SERVING:

- 5 whole wheat potato buns or gluten-free buns
- 10 butter lettuce leaves

1. For the lemon-caper rémoulade: In a small bowl, combine the mayonnaise, capers, parsley, and lemon juice and mix well.
2. For the salmon patties: Cut off a 4-ounce / 113-g piece of the salmon and transfer to a food processor. Pulse until it becomes pasty. With a sharp knife, chop the remaining salmon into small cubes.
3. In a medium bowl, combine the chopped and processed salmon with the panko, minced red onion, garlic, egg, mustard, lemon juice, parsley, and salt. Toss gently to combine. Form the mixture into 5 patties about ¾ inch thick. Refrigerate for at least 30 minutes.
4. Preheat the air fryer to 200°C.
5. Working in batches, place the patties in the baking pan. Bake for about 15 minutes, gently flipping halfway, until golden and cooked through.
6. To serve, transfer each patty to a bun. Top each with 2 lettuce leaves, 2 tablespoons of the rémoulade, and the slivered red onions.

Italian-Style Salmon Patties

Prep time: 10 minutes | Cook time: 8 minutes | Serves 4

- 2 (5-ounce / 142 g) cans salmon, flaked
- 2 large eggs, beaten
- ⅓ cup minced onion
- ⅔ cup panko bread crumbs
- 1½ teaspoons Italian-Style seasoning
- 1 teaspoon garlic powder
- Cooking spray

1. In a medium bowl, stir together the salmon, eggs, and onion.
2. In a small bowl, whisk the bread crumbs, Italian-Style seasoning, and garlic powder until blended. Add the bread crumb mixture to the salmon mixture and stir until blended. Shape the mixture into 8 patties.
3. Preheat the air fryer to 180°C. Line the baking pan with greaseproof paper.
4. Working in batches as needed, place the patties on the parchment and spritz with oil.
5. Bake for 4 minutes. Flip, spritz the patties with oil, and bake for 4 to 8 minutes more, until browned and firm. Serve.

Old Bay Salmon Patty Bites

Prep time: 15 minutes | Cook time: 15 minutes | Serves 4

- 4 (5-ounce / 142-g) cans pink salmon, skinless, boneless in water, drained
- 2 eggs, beaten
- 1 cup whole-wheat panko bread crumbs
- 4 tablespoons finely minced red bell pepper
- 2 tablespoons parsley flakes
- 2 teaspoons Old Bay seasoning
- Cooking spray

1. Preheat the air fryer to 200°C.
2. Spray the baking pan lightly with cooking spray.
3. In a medium bowl, mix the salmon, eggs, panko bread crumbs, red bell pepper, parsley flakes, and Old Bay seasoning.
4. Using a small biscuit scoop, form the mixture into 20 balls.
5. Place the salmon bites in the pan in a single layer and spray lightly with cooking spray. You may need to cook them in batches.
6. Bake for 15 minutes, stirring a couple of times for even cooking.
7. Serve immediately.

Garlic-Lemon Prawn

Prep time: 10 minutes | Cook time: 14 minutes | Serves 4

- 2 teaspoons minced garlic
- 2 teaspoons lemon juice
- 2 teaspoons olive oil
- ½ to 1 teaspoon crushed red pepper
- 12 ounces (340 g) medium Prawn, deveined, with tails on
- Cooking spray

1. In a medium bowl, mix together the garlic, lemon juice, olive oil, and crushed red pepper to make a marinade.
2. Add the Prawn and toss to coat in the marinade. Cover with Cling Film and place the bowl in the refrigerator for 30 minutes.
3. Preheat the air fryer to 200°C. Spray the baking pan lightly with cooking spray.
4. Place the Prawn in the pan. Bake for 6 minutes. Stir and bake until the Prawn are cooked through and nicely browned, an additional 8 minutes. Cool for 5 minutes before serving.

Trout Amandine with Lemon Butter Sauce

Prep time: 20 minutes | Cook time: 8 minutes | Serves 4

TROUT AMANDINE:

- ⅔ cup toasted almonds
- ⅓ cup grated Parmesan cheese
- 1 teaspoon salt
- ½ teaspoon freshly ground black pepper
- 2 tablespoons butter, melted
- 4 (4-ounce / 113-g) trout fillets, or salmon fillets
- Cooking spray

LEMON BUTTER SAUCE:

- 8 tablespoons (1 stick) butter, melted
- 2 tablespoons freshly squeezed lemon juice
- ½ teaspoon Worcestershire sauce
- ½ teaspoon salt
- ½ teaspoon freshly ground black pepper
- ¼ teaspoon chili sauce

1. In a blender or food processor, pulse the almonds for 5 to 10 seconds until finely processed. Transfer to a shallow bowl and whisk in the Parmesan cheese, salt, and pepper. Place the melted butter in another shallow bowl.
2. One at a time, dip the fish in the melted butter, then the almond mixture, coating thoroughly.
3. Preheat the air fryer to 150°C. Line the baking pan with greaseproof paper.
4. Place the coated fish on the parchment and spritz with oil.
5. Bake for 4 minutes. Flip the fish, spritz it with oil, and bake for 4 minutes more until the fish flakes easily with a fork.
6. In a small bowl, whisk the butter, lemon juice, Worcestershire sauce, salt, pepper, and chili sauce until blended.
7. Serve with the fish.

Parmesan Sriracha Tuna Patty Sliders

Prep time: 15 minutes | Cook time: 15 minutes | Serves 4

- 3 (5-ounce / 142-g) cans tuna, packed in water
- ⅔ cup whole-wheat panko bread crumbs
- ⅓ cup shredded Parmesan cheese
- 1 tablespoon sriracha
- ¾ teaspoon black pepper
- 10 whole-wheat slider buns
- Cooking spray

1. Preheat the air fryer to 190°C.
2. Spray the baking pan lightly with cooking spray.
3. In a medium bowl combine the tuna, bread crumbs, Parmesan cheese, sriracha, and black pepper and stir to combine.
4. Form the mixture into 10 patties.
5. Place the patties in the pan in a single layer. Spray the patties lightly with cooking spray. You may need to cook them in batches.
6. Bake for 8 minutes. Turn the patties over and lightly spray with cooking spray. Bake until golden brown and crisp, another 7 more minutes. Serve warm.

Paprika Tilapia with Garlic Aioli

Prep time: 5 minutes | Cook time: 15 minutes | Serves 4

TILAPIA:
- 4 tilapia fillets
- 1 tablespoon extra-virgin olive oil
- 1 teaspoon garlic powder
- 1 teaspoon paprika
- 1 teaspoon dried basil
- A pinch of lemon-pepper seasoning

GARLIC AIOLI:
- 2 garlic cloves, minced
- 1 tablespoon mayonnaise
- Juice of ½ lemon
- 1 teaspoon extra-virgin olive oil
- Salt and pepper, to taste

1. Preheat the air fryer to 200°C.
2. On a clean work surface, brush both sides of each fillet with the olive oil. Sprinkle with the garlic powder, paprika, basil, and lemon-pepper seasoning.
3. Place the fillets in the baking pan and bake for 15 minutes, flipping the fillets halfway through, or until the fish flakes easily and is no longer translucent in the center.
4. Meanwhile, make the garlic aioli: Whisk together the garlic, mayo, lemon juice, olive oil, salt, and pepper in a small bowl until smooth.
5. Remove the fish from the pan and serve with the garlic aioli on the side.

Mediterranean Baked Fish Fillet

Prep time: 10 minutes | Cook time: 25 minutes | Serves 4

- 4 (6-ounce / 170-g) fish fillets (red snapper, cod, whiting, sole, or mackerel)
- Mixture Ingredients:
- 1 tablespoon olive oil
- 2 tablespoons tomato purée
- 3 plum tomatoes, chopped
- 2 garlic cloves, minced
- 2 tablespoons capers
- 2 tablespoons pitted and chopped black olives
- 2 tablespoons chopped fresh basil leaves
- 2 tablespoons chopped fresh parsley

1. Combine the baking mixture ingredients in a small bowl. Set aside.
2. Layer the fillets in an oiled or nonstick square baking (cake) pan, overlapping them if necessary, and spoon the baking mixture over the fish.
3. Select Bake. Set temperature to 180°C and set time to 25 minutes. Select Start to begin preheating.
4. Once preheated, slide the pan into the oven.
5. When done, the fish will flake easily with a fork.

Curried Jewfish Fillets with Parmesan

Prep time: 5 minutes | Cook time: 10 minutes | Serves 4

- 2 medium-sized jewfish fillets
- Dash of tabasco sauce
- 1 teaspoon curry powder
- ½ teaspoon ground coriander
- ½ teaspoon hot paprika
- flake salt and freshly cracked mixed peppercorns, to taste
- 2 eggs
- 1½ tablespoons olive oil
- ½ cup grated Parmesan cheese

1. On a clean work surface, drizzle the jewfish fillets with the tabasco sauce. Sprinkle with the curry powder, coriander, hot paprika, salt, and cracked mixed peppercorns. Set aside.
2. In a shallow bowl, beat the eggs until frothy. In another shallow bowl, combine the olive oil and Parmesan cheese.
3. One at a time, dredge the jewfish fillets in the beaten eggs, shaking off any excess, then roll them over the Parmesan cheese until evenly coated.
4. Arrange the jewfish fillets in the perforated pan in a single layer.
5. Select Roast. Set temperature to 180°C and set time to 10 minutes. Press Start to begin preheating.
6. Once preheated, place the pan into the oven.
7. When cooking is complete, the fish should be golden brown and crisp. Cool for 5 minutes before serving.

Breaded Crab Cakes

Prep time: 10 minutes | Cook time: 30 minutes | Serves 6

- 1 pound (454 g) fresh lump crab meat, drained and chopped
- 1 cup bread crumbs
- ½ cup plain nonfat yogurt
- 1 tablespoon olive oil
- 2 tablespoons capers
- 1 tablespoon garlic powder
- 1 teaspoon chili sauce
- 1 egg, beaten
- 1 tablespoon Worcestershire sauce
- Salt and freshly ground black pepper, to taste

1. Combine all the ingredients in a bowl. Shape the mixture into patties approximately 2½ inches wide, adding more bread crumbs if the mixture is too wet and sticky and more yogurt if the mixture is too dry and crumbly. Place the patties in an oiled or nonstick square (cake) pan.
2. Select Bake. Set temperature to 180°C and set time to 25 minutes. Select Start to begin preheating.
3. Once preheated, slide the pan into the oven, uncovered.
4. After 25 minutes, select Broil Set temperature to 200°C and set time to 5 minutes.
5. When done, the patties will be golden brown.

Flounder Fillet and Asparagus Rolls

Prep time: 10 minutes | Cook time: 30 minutes | Serves 4

- 1 dozen asparagus stalks, tough stem part cut off
- 4 (6-ounce / 170-g) flounder fillets
- 4 tablespoons chopped scallions
- 4 tablespoons shredded carrots
- 4 tablespoons finely chopped
- Almonds
- 1 teaspoon dried dill weed
- Salt and freshly ground black pepper, to taste
- 1 lemon, cut into wedges

1. Place 3 asparagus stalks lengthwise on a flounder fillet. Add 1 tablespoon scallions, 1 tablespoon carrots, 1 tablespoon almonds, and a sprinkling of dill. Season to taste with salt and pepper and roll the fillet together so that the long edges overlap. Secure the edges with Cocktail Sticks or tie with cotton string. Carefully place the rolled fillet in an oiled or nonstick square baking (cake) pan. Repeat the process for the remaining ingredients. Cover the pan with tin foil .
2. Select Bake. Set temperature to 200°C and set time to 20 minutes. Select Start to begin preheating.
3. Once preheated, slide the pan into the oven, covered.
4. When done, the asparagus will be tender. Remove the cover.
5. Select Broil. Set temperature to 200°C and set time to 10 minutes. Slide the pan into the oven. When done, the fish will be lightly browned.
6. Remove and discard the Cocktail Sticks or string. Serve the rolled fillets with lemon wedges.

Stuffed Tilapia with Pepper and Cucumber

Prep time: 15 minutes | Cook time: 20 minutes | Makes 6 tilapia rolls

- 6 (5-ounce / 142-g) tilapia fillets
- 2 tablespoons olive oil

FILLING:

- 1 cucumber, peeled, seeds scooped out and discarded, and chopped
- ½ cup chopped roasted peppers, drained
- 2 tablespoons lemon juice
- 2 tablespoons chopped fresh parsley or Coriander
- 1 teaspoon garlic powder
- 1 teaspoon paprika
- Salt and freshly ground black pepper, to taste

DIP MIXTURE:

- 1 cup nonfat Soured cream
- 2 tablespoons low-fat mayonnaise
- 3 tablespoons Dijon mustard
- 1 teaspoon Worcestershire sauce
- 1 teaspoon dried dill

1. Combine the filling ingredients in a bowl, adjusting the seasonings to taste.
2. Spoon equal portions of filling in the centers of the tilapia filets. Roll up the fillets, starting at the smallest end. Secure each roll with Cocktail Sticks and place the rolls in an oiled or nonstick baking pan. Carefully brush the fillets with oil and place them in an oiled or nonstick square baking (cake) pan.
3. Select Broil. Set temperature to 200°C and set time to 20 minutes. Select Start to begin preheating.
4. Once preheated, slide the pan into the oven.
5. When done, the fillets will be lightly browned.
6. Combine the dip mixture ingredients in a small bowl and serve with the fish.

Chapter 7
Side Dishes

Air Fried Easy French chips

Prep Time: 7 minutes | Cooking Time: 9 minutes | Servings: 2

- 4 potatoes, peeled, cut
- ¼ tsp. Garlic powder
- ¼ tsp. salt
- 1 tsp. olive oil

1. Preheat your Air fryer to a temperature of 370°F for 5 minutes.
2. Sprinkle salt and garlic powder on potatoes and drizzle olive oil.
3. Put potatoes into the fryer basket and set time to 9 minutes.
4. Serve!

Air Fried Bok Choy

Prep time: 10 minutes | Cook time: 10 minutes | Serves 4

- 2 tablespoons olive oil
- 2 tablespoons coconut amino
- 2 teaspoons sesame oil
- 2 teaspoons chili-garlic sauce
- 2 cloves garlic, minced
- 1 head (about 1 pound / 454 g) bok choy, sliced lengthwise into quarters
- 2 teaspoons black sesame seeds

1. Preheat the Air fryer to 200°C.
2. In a large bowl, combine the olive oil, coconut amino, sesame oil, chili-garlic sauce, and garlic. Add the bok choy and toss, massaging the leaves with your hands if necessary, until thoroughly coated.
3. Arrange the bok choy in the air fryer basket or wire rack of the Air fryer. Pausing about halfway through the cooking time to shake the air fryer basket or wire rack, air fry for 7 to 10 minutes until the bok choy is tender and the tips of the leaves begin to crisp. Remove from the air fryer basket or wire rack and let cool for a few minutes before coarsely chopping. Serve sprinkled with the sesame seeds.

Brussels Sprout with Toasted Pecan

Prep time: 10 minutes | Cook time: 30 minutes | Serves 4

- ½ cup pecans
- 1½ pounds (680g) fresh Brussels sprouts, trimmed and quartered
- 2 tablespoons olive oil
- Salt and freshly ground black pepper
- ¼ cup crumbled Gorgonzola cheese

1. Spread the pecans in a single layer of the Air fryer and set the heat to 180°C. Air fry for 3 to 5 minutes until the pecans are lightly browned and fragrant. Transfer the pecans to a plate and continue preheating the Air fryer, increasing the heat to 200°C.
2. In a large bowl, toss the Brussels sprouts with the olive oil and season with salt and black pepper to taste.
3. Working in batches if necessary, arrange the Brussels sprouts in a single layer in the air fryer basket or wire rack. Pausing halfway through the baking time to shake the air fryer basket or wire rack, air fry for 20 to 25 minutes until the sprouts are tender and starting to brown on the edges.
4. Transfer the sprouts to a serving bowl and top with the toasted pecans and Gorgonzola. Serve warm or at room temperature.

Balsamic Brussels Sprout with Bacon

Prep time: 5 minutes | Cook time: 12 minutes | Serves 4

- 2 cups trimmed and halved fresh Brussels sprouts
- 2 tablespoons olive oil
- ¼ teaspoon salt
- ¼ teaspoon ground black pepper
- 2 tablespoons balsamic vinegar
- 2 slices cooked sugar-free bacon, crumbled

1. In a large bowl, toss Brussels sprouts in olive oil, then sprinkle with salt and pepper. Place into ungreased air fryer basket or wire rack. Adjust the temperature to 190°C (190°C) and set the timer for 12 minutes, shaking the air fryer basket or wire rack halfway through cooking. Brussels sprouts will be tender and browned when done.
2. Place sprouts in a large serving dish and drizzle with balsamic vinegar. Sprinkle bacon over top. Serve warm.

Roasted Cauliflower Florets

Prep Time: 6 minutes| Cooking Time: 12 minutes |Servings: 4

- 1 ½ lb. Cauliflower florets
- ½ tsp. Black pepper
- ¼ tsp. salt
- 1 tbsp. cooking oil

1. In a bowl, add cauliflower with cooking oil, salt, and pepper, toss well to combine.
2. Preheat your Air fryer to a temperature of 200°C.
3. Place cauliflower florets into the fryer basket and set time to 12 minutes.
4. After halftime, turn cauliflower florets so that they can cook evenly from both sides.
5. Serve!

Bacon-Wrapped Asparagus

Prep time: 5 minutes | Cook time: 10 minutes | Serves 4

- 8 slices reduced-sodium bacon, cut in half
- 16 thick (about 1 pound / 454 g) asparagus spears, trimmed of woody ends

1. Preheat the Air fryer to 180°C.
2. Wrap a half piece of bacon around the center of each stalk of asparagus.
3. Working in batches, if necessary, arrange seam-side down in a single layer in the air fryer basket or wire rack. Cook for 10 minutes until the bacon is crisp and the stalks are tender.

Kohlrabi chips

Prep time: 10 minutes | Cook time: 30 minutes | Serves 4

- 2 pounds (907 g) kohlrabi, peeled and cut into ¼–½-inch chips
- 2 tablespoons olive oil
- Salt and freshly ground black pepper

1. Preheat the Air fryer to 200°C.
2. In a large bowl, combine the kohlrabi and olive oil. Season to taste with salt and black pepper. Toss gently until thoroughly coated.
3. Working in batches if necessary, spread the kohlrabi in a single layer in the air fryer basket or wire rack. Pausing halfway through the cooking time to shake the air fryer basket or wire rack, air fry for 20 to 30 minutes until the chips are lightly browned and crunchy.

Air Fry Sweet Potato chips

Prep Time: 7 minutes | Cooking Time: 15 minutes | Servings: 3

- 1 medium Sweet potato
- 2 tbsp. Vegetable oil
- 1 tsp. Corn starch
- ¼ tsp. Salt

1. Wash and cut the sweet potatoes into a finger stick shape. Keep it at ¼" thickness.
2. Soak the cut sweet potato in a bowl of regular water for 30 minutes.
3. After that, drain the water and pat dry the potatoes.
4. Put it in a zip lock bag, add cornflour powder, and shake gently.
5. Layer the potatoes in the air fryer basket or wire rack.
6. Set the temperature of your Air fryer to 338°F and time to 15 minutes.
7. Shake while cooking in progress.
8. Sprinkle salt over it as required.
9. Serve hot.

Crispy Runner Beans

Prep time: 5 minutes | Cook time: 8 minutes | Serves 4

- 2 teaspoons olive oil
- ½ pound (227g) fresh Runner Beans, ends trimmed
- ¼ teaspoon salt
- ¼ teaspoon ground black pepper

1. In a large bowl, drizzle olive oil over Runner Beans and sprinkle with salt and pepper.
2. Place Runner Beans into ungreased air fryer basket or wire rack. Adjust the temperature to 180°C and set the timer for 8 minutes, shaking the air fryer basket or wire rack two times during cooking. Runner Beans will be dark golden and crispy at the edges when done. Serve warm.

Barbecue Parmesan Chicken Nuggets

Prep time: 20 minutes | Cook time: 12 minutes | Serves 6

- 1 pound (454 g) chicken breasts, slice into tenders
- ½ teaspoon cayenne pepper
- Salt and black pepper, to taste
- ¼ cup almond meal
- 1 egg, whisked
- ½ cup Parmesan cheese, freshly grated
- ¼ cup mayo
- ¼ cup no-sugar-added barbecue sauce

1. Pat the chicken tenders dry with a kitchen towel. Season with the cayenne pepper, salt, and black pepper.
2. Dip the chicken tenders into the almond meal, followed by the egg. Press the chicken tenders into the Parmesan cheese, coating evenly.
3. Place the chicken tenders in the lightly greased air fryer basket or wire rack. Cook at 360°F or 9 to 12 minutes, turning them over to cook evenly.
4. In a mixing bowl, thoroughly combine the mayonnaise with the barbecue sauce. Serve the chicken nuggets with the sauce for dipping. Bon appétit!

Chili Bacon-Wrapped Cabbage Bites

Prep time: 10 minutes | Cook time: 12 minutes | Serves 6

- 3 tablespoons hot chili sauce, divided
- 1 medium head cabbage, cored and cut into 12 bite-sized pieces
- 2 tablespoons coconut oil, melted
- ½ teaspoon salt
- 12 slices sugar-free bacon
- ½ cup mayonnaise
- ¼ teaspoon garlic powder

1. Evenly brush 2 tablespoons hot chili sauce onto cabbage pieces. Drizzle evenly with coconut oil, then sprinkle with salt.
2. Wrap each cabbage piece with bacon and secure with a toothpick. Place into ungreased air fryer basket or wire rack. Adjust the temperature to 190°C (190°C) and set the timer for 12 minutes, turning cabbage halfway through cooking. Bacon will be cooked and crispy when done.
3. In a small bowl, whisk together mayonnaise, garlic powder, and remaining chili sauce. Use as a dipping sauce for cabbage bites.

Cheesy Asparagus

Prep time: 10 minutes | Cook time: 18 minutes | Serves 4

- ½ cup heavy whipping cream
- ½ cup grated Parmesan cheese
- 2 ounces (57 g) cream cheese, softened
- 1 pound (454 g) asparagus, ends trimmed, chopped into 1-inch pieces
- ¼ teaspoon salt
- ¼ teaspoon ground black pepper

1. In a medium bowl, whisk together double cream, Parmesan, and cream cheese until combined.
2. Place asparagus into an ungreased 6-inch round nonstick baking dish. Pour cheese mixture over top and sprinkle with salt and pepper.
3. Place dish into air fryer basket or wire rack. Adjust the temperature to 180°C and set the timer for 18 minutes. Asparagus will be tender when done. Serve warm.

Air Fried Breaded Mushrooms

Prep Time: 9 minutes | Cooking Time: 7 minutes | Servings: 5

- ½ lb. button mushrooms
- 1 large Egg
- 3 oz. Grated cheese
- Breadcrumbs – as required to coat
- Flour – as necessary to coat
- ¼ tsp. Ground pepper
- ⅛ Tsp. Salt

1. In a bowl, mix well the bread crumbs with grated cheese then keep it aside.
2. Beat the egg in another bowl and keep it aside.
3. Wash the mushrooms and dry pat.
4. Put the flour on a flat surface then roll the mushroom in the flour.
5. Dip the flour rolled mushroom in the beaten egg.
6. Now dip the mushroom again in the cheese & bread crumb mixture.
7. Place the coated mushroom in the Air fryer cooking basket.
8. Set the temperature of your Air fryer at 180°C and time for 7 minutes.
9. Shake the air fryer basket or wire rack intermittently so that it can have an even frying.
10. Serve hot.

Courgette Fritters

Prep time: 15 minutes | Cook time: 10 minutes | Serves 4

- 2 courgette, grated (about 1 pound / 454 g)
- 1 teaspoon salt
- ¼ cup almond flour
- ¼ cup grated Parmesan cheese
- 1 large egg
- ¼ teaspoon dried thyme
- ¼ teaspoon ground turmeric
- ¼ teaspoon freshly ground black pepper
- 1 tablespoon olive oil
- ½ lemon, sliced into wedges

1. Preheat the Air fryer to 200°C. Cut a piece of greaseproof paper to fit slightly smaller than the bottom of the Air fryer.
2. Place the courgette in a large colander and sprinkle with the salt. Let sit for 5 to 10 minutes. Squeeze as much liquid as you can from the courgette and place in a large mixing bowl. Add the almond flour, Parmesan, egg, thyme, turmeric, and black pepper. Stir gently until thoroughly combined.
3. Shape the mixture into 8 patties and arrange on the greaseproof paper. Brush lightly with the olive oil. Pausing halfway through the cooking time to turn the patties, air fry for 10 minutes until golden brown. Serve warm with the lemon wedges.

Air Fried Courgette Salad

Prep time: 5 minutes | **Cook time:** 7 minutes | **Serves 4**

- 2 medium courgette, thinly sliced
- 5 tablespoons olive oil, divided
- ¼ cup chopped fresh parsley
- 2 tablespoons chopped fresh mint
- Zest and juice of ½ lemon
- 1 clove garlic, minced
- ¼ cup crumbled feta cheese
- Freshly ground black pepper

1. Preheat the Air fryer to 200°C.
2. In a large bowl, toss the courgette slices with 1 tablespoon of the olive oil.
3. Working in batches if necessary, arrange the courgette slices in an even layer in the air fryer basket or wire rack. Pausing halfway through the cooking time to shake the air fryer basket or wire rack, air fry for 5 to 7 minutes until soft and lightly browned on each side.
4. Meanwhile, in a small bowl, combine the remaining 4 tablespoons olive oil, parsley, mint, lemon zest, lemon juice, and garlic.
5. Arrange the courgette on a plate and drizzle with the dressing. Sprinkle the feta and black pepper on top. Serve warm or at room temperature.

Air Fryer Courgette Chips

Prep Time: 5 minutes | **Cooking Time:** 12 minutes | **Servings:** 4

1 cup breadcrumbs
1 medium courgette, thinly sliced
1 Egg
¾ cup Parmesan cheese, grated
Cooking spray – as required

1. Mix bread crumb, grated parmesan cheese in a medium bowl.
2. Beat egg in a medium bowl.
3. Set the Air fryer temperature to 180°C and preheat the Air fryer for 5 minutes.
4. Dip one courgette slice at a time in the beaten egg and dredge in the bread crumb mixture.
5. Press to coat and place in the air fryer basket or wire rack.
6. Repeat the process and place all courgette slices in the Air fryer side by side without overlapping.
7. Spray cooking oil slightly over the coated courgette.
8. Set the time to 10 minutes.
9. After 10 minutes, flip using a tong and cook again for 2 minutes.
10. Cook in batches.

Cauliflower with Lime Juice

Prep time: 10 minutes | Cook time: 7 minutes | Serves 4

- 2 cups chopped cauliflower florets
- 2 tablespoons coconut oil, melted
- 2 teaspoons chili powder
- ½ teaspoon garlic powder
- 1 medium lime
- 2 tablespoons chopped Coriander

1. In a large bowl, toss cauliflower with coconut oil. Sprinkle with chili powder and garlic powder. Place seasoned cauliflower into the air fryer basket or wire rack.
2. Adjust the temperature to 180°C and set the timer for 7 minutes.
3. Cauliflower will be tender and begin to turn golden at the edges. Place into serving bowl.
4. Cut the lime into quarters and squeeze juice over cauliflower. Garnish with Coriander.

Double Cheese Roasted Asparagus

Prep time: 5 minutes | Cook time: 10 minutes | Serves 4

- ⅔ pound (302 g) asparagus spears, of medium thickness
- Extra-virgin olive oil
- Sea salt flakes and freshly ground black pepper, to taste
- 4½ ounces (127 g) ricotta cheese (fresh rather than ultra-pasteurized, if possible)
- Pecorino cheese, or Parmesan cheese, shaved

1. Trim the woody ends from the asparagus spears, put them on an sheet pan with a slight lip, and drizzle with olive oil. Season with salt.
2. Select Bake. Set temperature to 200°C and set time to 10 minutes. Select Start to begin preheating.
3. Once preheated, slide the pan into the Air Fryer.
4. When done, the asparagus spears will be tender.
5. Put the asparagus on a serving plate. Scatter the ricotta in nuggets over the top, followed by the shaved pecorino or Parmesan cheese. Season with salt and pepper, pour on more olive oil, and serve immediately.

Golden Potato, Carrot and Onion

Prep time: 10 minutes | Cook time: 38 minutes | Serves 4

- 2 cups peeled and shredded potatoes
- ½ cup peeled and shredded carrots
- ¼ cup shredded onion
- 1 teaspoon salt
- 1 teaspoon dried rosemary
- 1 teaspoon dried cumin
- 3 tablespoons vegetable oil
- Salt and freshly ground black pepper, to taste

1. Mix all the ingredients together in an ovenproof baking dish. Adjust the seasonings to taste. Cover the dish with tin foil.
2. Select Bake. Set temperature to 200°C and set time to 30 minutes. Select Start to begin preheating.
3. Once preheated, slide the baking dish into the Air Fryer. When done, the vegetables will be tender. Remove the cover.
4. Select Broil. Set temperature to 200°C and set time to 8 minutes. Slide the pan into the Air Fryer. When done, the top will be browned.

Potato Shells with Cheddar and Bacon

Prep time: 5 minutes | Cook time: 8 minutes | Serves 4

- 4 tablespoons shredded reduced-fat Cheddar cheese
- 4 slices lean turkey bacon, cooked and crumbled
- 4 potato shells
- 4 tablespoons nonfat Soured cream
- 4 teaspoons chopped fresh or frozen chives
- Salt and freshly ground black pepper, to taste

1. Sprinkle 1 tablespoon Cheddar cheese and 1 tablespoon crumbled bacon into each potato shell. Place the shells on a broiling rack with a pan underneath.
2. Select Broil. Set temperature to 200°C and set time to 8 minutes. Select Start to begin preheating.
3. Once preheated, slide the pan into the Air Fryer.
4. When done, the cheese will be melted and the shells lightly browned. Spoon 1 tablespoon Soured cream into each shell and sprinkle with 1 teaspoon chives. Add salt and pepper to taste.

Butternut marrow and Parsnip with Thyme

Prep time: 5 minutes | Cook time: 16 minutes | Serves 2

- 1 parsnip, sliced
- 1 cup sliced butternut marrow
- 1 small red onion, cut into wedges
- ½ chopped celery stalk
- 1 tablespoon chopped fresh thyme
- 2 teaspoons olive oil
- Salt and black pepper, to taste

1. Toss all the ingredients in a large bowl until the vegetables are well coated.
2. Transfer the vegetables to the perforated pan.
3. Select Air Fry. Set temperature to 190°C and set time to 16 minutes. Press Start to begin preheating.
4. Once preheated, place the pan into the Air Fryer. Stir the vegetables halfway through the cooking time.
5. When cooking is complete, the vegetables should be golden brown and tender. Remove from the Air Fryer and serve warm.

Ginger-Pepper Broccoli

Prep time: 5 minutes | Cook time: 10 minutes | Serves 2

- 12 ounces (340 g) broccoli florets
- 2 tablespoons Asian hot chili oil
- 1 teaspoon ground Sichuan peppercorns (or black pepper)
- 2 garlic cloves, finely chopped
- 1 (2-inch) piece fresh ginger, peeled and finely chopped
- flake salt and freshly ground black pepper

1. Toss the broccoli florets with the chili oil, Sichuan peppercorns, garlic, ginger, salt, and pepper in a mixing bowl until thoroughly coated.
2. Transfer the broccoli florets to the perforated pan.
3. Select Air Fry. Set temperature to 190°C and set time to 10 minutes. Press Start to begin preheating.
4. Once preheated, place the pan into the Air Fryer. Stir the broccoli florets halfway through the cooking time.
5. When cooking is complete, the broccoli florets should be lightly browned and tender. Remove the broccoli from the Air Fryer and serve on a plate.

Chapter 8
Casseroles, Frittata, and Quiche

Broccoli, Carrot, and Tomato Quiche

Prep time: 6 minutes | **Cook time:** 14 minutes | **Serves 4**

- 4 eggs
- 1 teaspoon dried thyme
- 1 cup whole milk
- 1 steamed carrots, diced
- 2 cups steamed broccoli florets
- 2 medium tomatoes, diced
- ¼ cup crumbled feta cheese
- 1 cup grated Cheddar cheese
- 1 teaspoon chopped parsley
- Salt and ground black pepper, to taste
- Cooking spray

1. Spritz a baking pan with cooking spray.
2. Whisk together the eggs, thyme, salt, and ground black pepper in a bowl and fold in the milk while mixing.
3. Put the carrots, broccoli, and tomatoes in the prepared baking pan, then spread with feta cheese and ½ cup Cheddar cheese. Pour the egg mixture over, then scatter with remaining Cheddar on top.
4. Slide the pan into the air fryer. Press the Power Button. Cook at 180°C for 14 minutes.
5. When cooking is complete, the egg should be set and the quiche should be puffed.
6. Remove the quiche from the air fryer and top with chopped parsley, then slice to serve.

Burgundy Beef and Mushroom Casserole

Prep time: 10 minutes | **Cook time:** 25 minutes | **Serves 4**

- 1½ pounds (680 g) beef steak
- 1 ounce (28 g) dry onion soup mix
- 2 cups sliced mushrooms
- 1 (14.5-ounce / 411-g) can cream of mushroom soup
- ½ cup beef broth
- ¼ cup red wine
- 3 garlic cloves, minced
- 1 whole onion, chopped

1. Put the beef steak in a large bowl, then sprinkle with dry onion soup mix. Toss to coat well.
2. Combine the mushrooms with mushroom soup, beef broth, red wine, garlic, and onion in a large bowl. Stir to mix well.
3. Transfer the beef steak to a baking pan, then pour in the mushroom mixture.
4. Slide the pan into the air fryer. Press the Power Button. Cook at 180°C for 25 minutes.
5. When cooking is complete, the mushrooms should be soft and the beef should be well browned.
6. Remove the baking pan from the air fryer and serve immediately.

Cauliflower and Pumpkin Casserole

Prep time: 15 minutes | **Cook time:** 50 minutes | **Serves 6**

- 1 cup chicken broth
- 2 cups cauliflower florets
- 1 cup tinned pumpkin purée
- ¼ cup double cream
- 1 teaspoon vanilla extract
- 2 large eggs, beaten
- ⅓ cup unsalted butter, melted, plus more for greasing the pan
- ¼ cup sugar
- 1 teaspoon fine sea salt
- Chopped fresh parsley leaves, for garnish
- Topping:
- ½ cup blanched almond flour
- 1 cup chopped pecans
- ⅓ cup unsalted butter, melted
- ½ cup sugar

1. Pour the chicken broth in a baking pan, then add the cauliflower.
2. Slide the pan into the air fryer. Press the Power Button. Cook at 180°C for 20 minutes.
3. When cooking is complete, the cauliflower should be soft.
4. Meanwhile, combine the ingredients for the topping in a large bowl. Stir to mix well.
5. Pat the cauliflower dry with kitchen paper, then place in a food processor and pulse with pumpkin purée, double cream, vanilla extract, eggs, butter, sugar, and salt until smooth.
6. Clean the baking pan and grease with more butter, then pour the purée mixture in the pan. Spread the topping over the mixture.
7. Place the baking pan back to the air fryer. Cook for 30 minutes.
8. When baking is complete, the topping of the casserole should be lightly browned.
9. Remove the casserole from the air fryer and serve with fresh parsley on top.

Chicken Divan

Prep time: 5 minutes | **Cook time:** 24 minutes | **Serves 4**

- 4 chicken breasts
- Salt and ground black pepper, to taste
- 1 head broccoli, cut into florets
- ½ cup cream of mushroom soup
- 1 cup shredded Cheddar cheese
- ½ cup croutons
- Cooking spray

1. Spritz the air flow racks with cooking spray.
2. Put the chicken breasts in the air flow racks and sprinkle with salt and ground black pepper.
3. Slide the racks into the air fryer. Press the Power Button. Cook at 200°C for 14 minutes.
4. Flip the breasts halfway through the cooking time.
5. When cooking is complete, the breasts should be well browned and tender.
6. Remove the breasts from the air fryer and allow to cool for a few minutes on a plate, then cut the breasts into bite-size pieces.
7. Combine the chicken, broccoli, mushroom soup, and Cheddar cheese in a large bowl. Stir to mix well.
8. Spritz a baking pan with cooking spray. Pour the chicken mixture into the pan. Spread the croutons over the mixture.
9. Set time to 10 minutes. Place the pan into the air fryer.
10. When cooking is complete, the croutons should be lightly browned and the mixture should be set.
11. Remove the baking pan from the air fryer and serve immediately.

Chicken Ham Casserole

Prep time: 15 minutes | Cook time: 15 minutes | Serves 4 to 6

- 2 cups diced cooked chicken
- 1 cup diced ham
- ¼ teaspoon ground nutmeg
- ½ cup half-and-half
- ½ teaspoon ground black pepper
- 6 slices Emmethaler
- Cooking spray

1. Spritz a baking pan with cooking spray.
2. Combine the chicken, ham, nutmeg, half-and-half, and ground black pepper in a large bowl. Stir to mix well.
3. Pour half of the mixture into the baking pan, then top the mixture with 3 slices of Emmethaler, then pour in the remaining mixture and top with remaining cheese slices.
4. Slide the pan into the air fryer. Press the Power Button. Cook at 180°C for 15 minutes.
5. When cooking is complete, the egg should be set and the cheese should be melted.
6. Serve immediately.

Chicken banger and Broccoli Casserole

Prep time: 10 minutes | Cook time: 20 minutes | Serves 8

- 10 eggs
- 1 cup Cheddar cheese, shredded and divided
- ¾ cup heavy whipping cream
- 1 (12-ounce / 340-g) package cooked chicken banger
- 1 cup broccoli, chopped
- 2 cloves garlic, minced
- ½ tablespoon salt
- ¼ tablespoon ground black pepper
- Cooking spray

1. Spritz a baking pan with cooking spray.
2. Whisk the eggs with Cheddar and cream in a large bowl to mix well.
3. Combine the cooked banger, broccoli, garlic, salt, and ground black pepper in a separate bowl. Stir to mix well.
4. Pour the banger mixture into the baking pan, then spread the egg mixture over to cover.
5. Slide the pan into the air fryer. Press the Power Button. Cook at 200°C for 20 minutes.
6. When cooking is complete, the egg should be set and a toothpick inserted in the center should come out clean.
7. Serve immediately.

Chorizo, Corn, and Potato Frittata

Prep time: 8 minutes | Cook time: 12 minutes | Serves 4

- 2 tablespoons olive oil
- 1 chorizo, sliced
- 4 eggs
- ½ cup corn
- 1 large potato, boiled and cubed
- 1 tablespoon chopped parsley
- ½ cup feta cheese, crumbled
- Salt and ground black pepper, to taste

1. Heat the olive oil in a nonstick frying pan over medium heat until shimmering.
2. Add the chorizo and cook for 4 minutes or until golden brown.
3. Whisk the eggs in a bowl, then sprinkle with salt and ground black pepper.
4. Mix the remaining ingredients in the egg mixture, then pour the chorizo and its fat into a baking pan. Pour in the egg mixture.
5. Slide the pan into the air fryer. Press the Power Button. Cook at 170°C for 8 minutes.
6. Stir the mixture halfway through.
7. When cooking is complete, the eggs should be set.
8. Serve immediately.

Goat Cheese and Asparagus Frittata

Prep time: 5 minutes | Cook time: 25 minutes | Serves 2 to 4

- 1 cup asparagus spears, cut into 1-inch pieces
- 1 teaspoon vegetable oil
- 1 tablespoon milk
- 6 eggs, beaten
- 2 ounces (57 g) goat cheese, crumbled
- 1 tablespoon minced chives, optional
- flake salt and pepper, to taste

1. Add the asparagus spears to a small bowl and drizzle with the vegetable oil. Toss until well coated and transfer to the air flow racks.
2. Slide the racks into the air fryer. Press the Power Button. Cook at 200°C for 5 minutes.
3. Flip the asparagus halfway through.
4. When cooking is complete, the asparagus should be tender and slightly wilted.
5. Remove the racks from the air fryer. Transfer the asparagus to a baking pan.
6. Stir together the milk and eggs in a medium bowl. Pour the mixture over the asparagus in the pan. Sprinkle with the goat cheese and the chives (if using) over the eggs. Season with salt and pepper.
7. Slide the pan into the air fryer. Press the Power Button. Cook at 160°C for 20 minutes. Press Start.
8. When cooking is complete, the top should be golden and the eggs should be set.
9. Transfer to a serving dish. Slice and serve.

Riced Cauliflower Casserole

Prep time: 8 minutes | Cook time: 12 minutes | Serves 4

- 1 head cauliflower, cut into florets
- 1 cup okra, chopped
- 1 yellow bell pepper, chopped
- 2 eggs, beaten
- ½ cup chopped onion
- 1 tablespoon soy sauce
- 2 tablespoons olive oil
- Salt and ground black pepper, to taste

1. Spritz a baking pan with cooking spray.
2. Put the cauliflower in a food processor and pulse to rice the cauliflower.
3. Pour the cauliflower rice in the baking pan and add the remaining ingredients. Stir to mix well.
4. Slide the pan into the air fryer. Press the Power Button. Cook at 190°C for 12 minutes.
5. When cooking is complete, the eggs should be set.
6. Remove the baking pan from the air fryer and serve immediately.

Banger and Colourful Peppers Casserole

Prep time: 15 minutes | Cook time: 25 minutes | Serves 6

- 1 pound (454 g) minced breakfast banger
- 1 yellow pepper, diced
- 1 red pepper, diced
- 1 green pepper, diced
- 1 sweet onion, diced
- 2 cups Cheddar cheese, shredded
- 6 eggs
- Salt and freshly ground black pepper, to taste
- Fresh parsley, for garnish

1. Cook the banger in a nonstick frying pan over medium heat for 10 minutes or until well browned. Stir constantly.
2. When the cooking is finished, transfer the cooked banger to a baking pan and add the peppers and onion. Scatter with Cheddar cheese.
3. Whisk the eggs with salt and ground black pepper in a large bowl, then pour the mixture into the baking pan.
4. Slide the pan into the air fryer. Press the Power Button. Cook at 180°C for 15 minutes.
5. When cooking is complete, the egg should be set and the edges of the casserole should be lightly browned.
6. Remove the baking pan from the air fryer and top with fresh parsley before serving.

Prawn Spinach Frittata

Prep time: 6 minutes | Cook time: 14 minutes | Serves 4

- 4 whole eggs
- 1 teaspoon dried basil
- ½ cup Prawn, cooked and chopped
- ½ cup baby spinach
- ½ cup rice, cooked
- ½ cup Parmesan Cheese, grated
- Salt, to taste
- Cooking spray

1. Spritz a baking pan with cooking spray.
2. Whisk the eggs with basil and salt in a large bowl until bubbly, then mix in the Prawn, spinach, rice, and cheese.
3. Pour the mixture into the baking pan.
4. Slide the pan into the air fryer. Press the Power Button. Cook at 180°C for 14 minutes.
5. Stir the mixture halfway through.
6. When cooking is complete, the eggs should be set and the frittata should be golden brown.
7. Slice to serve.

Smoked Trout and Crème Fraiche Frittata

Prep time: 8 minutes | Cook time: 17 minutes | Serves 4

- 2 tablespoons olive oil
- 1 onion, sliced
- 1 egg, beaten
- ½ tablespoon horseradish sauce
- 6 tablespoons crème fraiche
- 1 cup diced smoked trout
- 2 tablespoons chopped fresh dill
- Cooking spray

1. Spritz a baking pan with cooking spray.
2. Heat the olive oil in a nonstick frying pan over medium heat until shimmering.
3. Add the onion and sauté for 3 minutes or until translucent.
4. Combine the egg, horseradish sauce, and crème fraiche in a large bowl. Stir to mix well, then mix in the sautéed onion, smoked trout, and dill.
5. Pour the mixture in the prepared baking pan.
6. Slide the pan into the air fryer. Press the Power Button. Cook at 180°C for 14 minutes.
7. Stir the mixture halfway through.
8. When cooking is complete, the egg should be set and the edges should be lightly browned.
9. Serve immediately.

Spinach and Chickpea Casserole

Prep time: 10 minutes | **Cook time:** 21 to 22 minutes | **Serves 4**

- 2 tablespoons olive oil
- 2 garlic cloves, minced
- 1 tablespoon ginger, minced
- 1 onion, chopped
- 1 chili pepper, minced
- Salt and ground black pepper, to taste
- 1 pound (454 g) spinach
- 1 can coconut milk
- ½ cup dried tomatoes, chopped
- 1 (14-ounce / 397-g) can chickpeas, drained

1. Heat the olive oil in a saucepan over medium heat. Sauté the garlic and ginger in the olive oil for 1 minute, or until fragrant.
2. Add the onion, chili pepper, salt and pepper to the saucepan. Sauté for 3 minutes.
3. Mix in the spinach and sauté for 3 to 4 minutes or until the vegetables become soft. Remove from heat.
4. Pour the vegetable mixture into a baking pan. Stir in coconut milk, dried tomatoes and chickpeas until well blended.
5. Slide the pan into the air fryer. Press the Power Button. Cook at 190°C for 15 minutes.
6. When cooking is complete, transfer the casserole to a serving dish. Let cool for 5 minutes before serving.

Cauliflower Casserole with Pecan Butter

Prep time: 15 minutes | **Cook time:** 50 minutes | **Serves 6**

- 1 cup chicken broth
- 2 cups cauliflower florets
- 1 cup tinned pumpkin purée
- ¼ cup double cream
- 1 teaspoon vanilla extract
- 2 large eggs, beaten
- ⅓ cup unsalted butter, melted, plus more for greasing the pan
- ¼ cup sugar
- 1 teaspoon fine sea salt
- Chopped fresh parsley leaves, for garnish
- Topping:
- ½ cup blanched almond flour
- 1 cup chopped pecans
- ⅓ cup unsalted butter, melted
- ½ cup sugar

1. Pour the chicken broth in a baking pan, then add the cauliflower.
2. Select Bake. Set temperature to 180°C and set time to 20 minutes. Press Start to begin preheating.
3. Once preheated, place the pan into the oven.
4. When cooking is complete, the cauliflower should be soft.
5. Meanwhile, combine the ingredients for the topping in a large bowl. Stir to mix well.
6. Pat the cauliflower dry with kitchen paper, then place in a food processor and pulse with pumpkin purée, double cream, vanilla extract, eggs, butter, sugar, and salt until smooth.
7. Clean the baking pan and grease with more butter, then pour the purée mixture in the pan. Spread the topping over the mixture.
8. Place the baking pan back to the oven. Select Bake and set time to 30 minutes.
9. When baking is complete, the topping of the casserole should be lightly browned.
10. Remove the casserole from the oven and serve with fresh parsley on top.

Cheddar Chicken banger Casserole

Prep time: 10 minutes | Cook time: 20 minutes | Serves 8

- 10 eggs
- 1 cup Cheddar cheese, shredded and divided
- ¾ cup heavy whipping cream
- 1 (12-ounce / 340-g) package cooked chicken banger
- 1 cup broccoli, chopped
- 2 cloves garlic, minced
- ½ tablespoon salt
- ¼ tablespoon ground black pepper
- Cooking spray

1. Spritz a baking pan with cooking spray.
2. Whisk the eggs with Cheddar and cream in a large bowl to mix well.
3. Combine the cooked banger, broccoli, garlic, salt, and ground black pepper in a separate bowl. Stir to mix well.
4. Pour the banger mixture into the baking pan, then spread the egg mixture over to cover.
5. Select Bake. Set temperature to 200°C and set time to 20 minutes. Press Start to begin preheating.
6. Once preheated, place the pan into the oven.
7. When cooking is complete, the egg should be set and a toothpick inserted in the center should come out clean.
8. Serve immediately.

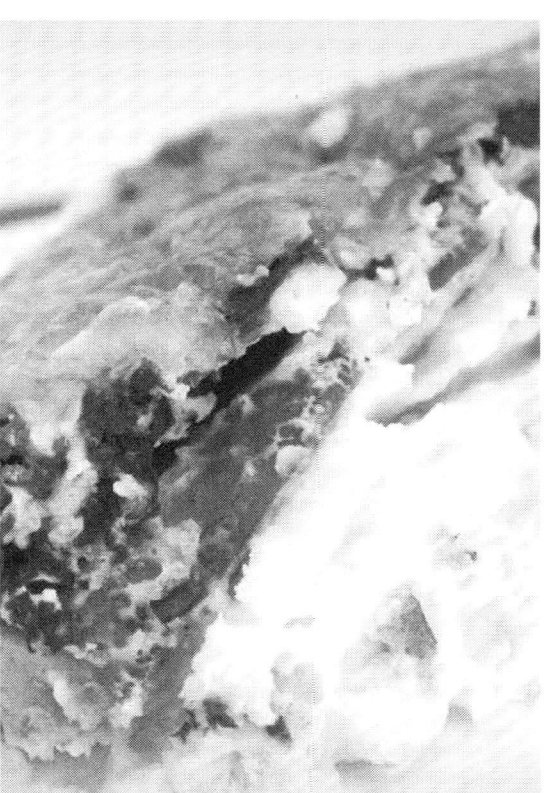

Corn Casserole with Bell Pepper

Prep time: 10 minutes | Cook time: 20 minutes | Serves 4

- 1 cup corn kernels
- ¼ cup bell pepper, finely chopped
- ½ cup low-fat milk
- 1 large egg, beaten
- ½ cup yellow cornmeal
- ½ cup plain flour
- ½ teaspoon baking powder
- 2 tablespoons melted unsalted butter
- 1 tablespoon granulated sugar
- Pinch of cayenne pepper
- ¼ teaspoon flaked salt
- Cooking spray

1. Spritz a baking pan with cooking spray.
2. Combine all the ingredients in a large bowl. Stir to mix well. Pour the mixture into the baking pan.
3. Select Bake. Set temperature to 170°C and set time to 20 minutes. Press Start to begin preheating.
4. Once preheated, place the pan into the oven.
5. When cooking is complete, the casserole should be lightly browned and set.
6. Remove the baking pan from the oven and serve immediately.

Asparagus Casserole with corn meal
Prep time: 5 minutes | Cook time: 30 minutes | Serves 4

- 10 fresh asparagus spears, cut into 1-inch pieces
- 2 cups cooked corn meal, cooled to room temperature
- 2 teaspoons Worcestershire sauce
- 1 egg, beaten
- ½ teaspoon garlic powder
- ¼ teaspoon salt
- 2 slices provolone cheese, crushed
- Cooking spray

1. Spritz a baking pan with cooking spray.
2. Set the asparagus in the perforated pan. Spritz the asparagus with cooking spray.
3. Select Air Fry. Set temperature to 200°C and set time to 5 minutes. Press Start to begin preheating.
4. Once preheated, place the pan into the oven. Flip the asparagus halfway through.
5. When cooking is complete, the asparagus should be lightly browned and crispy.
6. Meanwhile, combine the corn meal, Worcestershire sauce, egg, garlic powder, and salt in a bowl. Stir to mix well.
7. Pour half of the corn meal mixture in the prepared baking pan, then spread with fried asparagus.
8. Spread the cheese over the asparagus and pour the remaining corn meal over.
9. Select Bake. Set time to 25 minutes. Place the pan into the oven.
10. When cooking is complete, the egg should be set.
11. Serve immediately.

Cheddar Broccoli Casserole
Prep time: 5 minutes | Cook time: 30 minutes | Serves 6

- 4 cups broccoli florets
- ¼ cup heavy whipping cream
- ½ cup sharp Cheddar cheese, shredded
- ¼ cup ranch dressing
- flake salt and ground black pepper, to taste

1. Combine all the ingredients in a large bowl. Toss to coat well broccoli well.
2. Pour the mixture into a baking pan.
3. Select Bake. Set temperature to 190°C and set time to 30 minutes. Press Start to begin preheating.
4. Once preheated, place the pan into the oven.
5. When cooking is complete, the broccoli should be tender.
6. Remove the baking pan from the oven and serve immediately.

Tilapia and Rockfish Casserole
Prep time: 8 minutes | Cook time: 22 minutes | Serves 2

- 1 tablespoon olive oil
- 1 small yellow onion, chopped
- 2 garlic cloves, minced
- 4 ounces (113 g) tilapia pieces
- 4 ounces (113 g) rockfish pieces
- ½ teaspoon dried basil
- Salt and ground white pepper, to taste
- 4 eggs, lightly beaten
- 1 tablespoon dry sherry
- 4 tablespoons cheese, shredded

1. Heat the olive oil in a nonstick frying pan over medium-high heat until shimmering.
2. Add the onion and garlic and sauté for 2 minutes or until fragrant.
3. Add the tilapia, rockfish, basil, salt, and white pepper to the frying pan. Sauté to combine well and transfer them on a baking pan.
4. Combine the eggs, sherry and cheese in a large bowl. Stir to mix well. Pour the mixture in the baking pan over the fish mixture.
5. Select Bake. Set temperature to 180°C and set time to 20 minutes. Press Start to begin preheating.
6. Once preheated, place the pan into the oven.
7. When cooking is complete, the eggs should be set and the casserole edges should be lightly browned.
8. Serve immediately.

Blueberry and Peach Galette

Prep time: 10 minutes | Cook time: 20 minutes | Serves 6

- 1 pint blueberries, rinsed and picked through (about 2 cups)
- 2 large peaches or nectarines, peeled and cut into ½-inch slices (about 2 cups)
- ⅓ cup plus 2 tablespoons granulated sugar, divided
- 2 tablespoons unbleached plain flour
- ½ teaspoon grated lemon zest (optional)
- ¼ teaspoon ground allspice or cinnamon
- Pinch kosher or fine salt
- 1 (9-inch) refrigerated piecrust (or use homemade)
- 2 teaspoons unsalted butter, cut into pea-size pieces
- 1 large egg, beaten

1. Mix the blueberries, peaches, ⅓ cup of sugar, flour, lemon zest (if desired), allspice, and salt in a medium bowl.
2. Unroll the crust on a sheet pan, patching any tears if needed. Place the fruit in the center of the crust, leaving about 1½ inches of space around the edges. Scatter the butter pieces over the fruit. Fold the outside edge of the crust over the outer circle of the fruit, making pleats as needed.
3. Brush the egg over the crust. Sprinkle the crust and fruit with the remaining 2 tablespoons of sugar.
4. Slide the pan into the air fryer. Press the Power Button. Cook at 180°C for 20 minutes.
5. After about 15 minutes, check the galette, rotating the pan if the crust is not browning evenly. Continue cooking until the crust is deep golden brown and the fruit is bubbling.
6. When cooking is complete, remove from the air fryer and allow to cool for 10 minutes before slicing and serving.

Breaded Bananas with Chocolate Sauce

Prep time: 10 minutes | Cook time: 7 minutes | Serves 6

- ¼ cup cornflour
- ¼ cup plain bread crumbs
- 1 large egg, beaten
- 3 bananas, halved crosswise
- Cooking spray
- Chocolate sauce, for serving

1. Place the cornflour, bread crumbs, and egg in three separate bowls.
2. Roll the bananas in the cornflour, then in the beaten egg, and finally in the bread crumbs to coat well.
3. Spritz the air flow racks with cooking spray.
4. Arrange the banana halves in the air flow racks and mist them with cooking spray.
5. Slide the racks into the air fryer. Press the Power Button. Cook at 180°C for 7 minutes.
6. After about 5 minutes, flip the bananas and continue to cook for another 2 minutes.
7. When cooking is complete, remove the bananas from the air fryer to a serving plate. Serve with the chocolate sauce drizzled over the top.

Chapter 9
Desserts

Caramelized Fruit Kebabs

Prep time: 10 minutes | Cook time: 4 minutes | Serves 4

- 2 peaches, peeled, pitted, and thickly sliced
- 3 plums, halved and pitted
- 3 nectarines, halved and pitted
- 1 tablespoon honey
- ½ teaspoon ground cinnamon
- ¼ teaspoon ground allspice
- Pinch cayenne pepper

SPECIAL EQUIPMENT:
- 8 metal skewers

1. Thread, alternating peaches, plums, and nectarines onto the metal skewers that fit into the air fryer.
2. Thoroughly combine the honey, cinnamon, allspice, and cayenne in a small bowl. Brush generously the glaze over the fruit skewers.
3. Transfer the fruit skewers to the air flow racks.
4. Slide the racks into the air fryer. Press the Power Button. Cook at 200°C for 4 minutes.
5. When cooking is complete the fruit should be caramelized.
6. Remove the fruit skewers from the air fryer and let rest for 5 minutes before serving.

Caramelized Pear Tart

Prep time: 15 minutes | Cook time: 25 minutes | Serves 8

- Juice of 1 lemon
- 4 cups water
- 3 medium or 2 large ripe or almost ripe pears (preferably Bosc or Anjou), peeled, stemmed, and halved lengthwise
- 1 sheet (½ package) frozen puff pastry, thawed
- plain flour, for dusting
- 4 tablespoons caramel sauce such as Smucker's Salted Caramel, divided

1. Combine the lemon juice and water in a large bowl.
2. Remove the seeds from the pears with a melon baller and cut out the blossom end. Remove any tough fibers between the stem end and the center. As you work, place the pear halves in the acidulated water.
3. On a lightly floured cutting board, unwrap and unfold the puff pastry, roll it lightly with a rolling pin to press the folds together. Place it on a sheet pan.
4. Roll about ½ inch of the pastry edges up to form a ridge around the perimeter. Crimp the corners together to create a solid rim around the pastry to hold in the liquid as the tart cooks.
5. Brush 2 tablespoons of caramel sauce over the bottom of the pastry.
6. Remove the pear halves from the water and blot off any remaining water with kitchen paper.
7. Place one of the halves on the board cut-side down and cut ¼-inch-thick slices radially. Repeat with the remaining halves. Arrange the pear slices over the pastry. Drizzle the remaining 2 tablespoons of caramel sauce over the top.
8. Slide the pan into the air fryer. Press the Power Button. Cook at 180°C for 25 minutes.
9. After 15 minutes, check the tart, rotating the pan if the crust is not browning evenly. Continue cooking for another 10 minutes, or until the pastry is golden brown, the pears are soft, and the caramel is bubbling.
10. When done, remove from the air fryer and allow to cool for about 10 minutes.
11. Served warm.

Peach-Blueberry Tart

Prep time: 10 minutes | Cook time: 30 minutes | Serves 6 to 8

- 4 peaches, pitted and sliced
- 1 cup fresh blueberries
- 2 tablespoons cornflour
- 3 tablespoons sugar
- 1 tablespoon freshly squeezed lemon juice
- Cooking spray
- 1 sheet frozen puff pastry, thawed
- 1 tablespoon nonfat or low-fat milk
- Confectioners' sugar, for dusting

1. Add the peaches, blueberries, cornflour, sugar, and lemon juice to a large bowl and toss to coat.
2. Spritz a round baking pan with cooking spray.
3. Unfold the pastry and put on the prepared baking pan.
4. Lay the peach slices on the pan, slightly overlapping them. Scatter the blueberries over the peach.
5. Drape the pastry over the outside of the fruit and press pleats firmly together. Brush the milk over the pastry.
6. Slide the pan into the air fryer. Press the Power Button. Cook at 200°C for 30 minutes.
7. Bake Cook until the crust is golden brown and the fruit is bubbling.
8. When cooking is complete, remove from the air fryer and allow to cool for 10 minutes.
9. Serve the tart with the confectioners' sugar sprinkled on top.

Peanut Butter-Chocolate Bread Pudding

Prep time: 10 minutes | Cook time: 10 minutes | Serves 8

- 1 egg
- 1 egg yolk
- ¾ cup chocolate milk
- 3 tablespoons Demerara sugar
- 3 tablespoons peanut butter
- 2 tablespoons cocoa powder
- 1 teaspoon vanilla
- 5 slices firm white bread, cubed
- Nonstick cooking spray

1. Spritz a baking pan with nonstick cooking spray.
2. Whisk together the egg, egg yolk, chocolate milk, Demerara sugar, peanut butter, cocoa powder, and vanilla until well combined.
3. Fold in the bread cubes and stir to mix well. Allow the bread soak for 10 minutes.
4. When ready, transfer the egg mixture to the prepared baking pan.
5. Slide the pan into the air fryer. Press the Power Button. Cook at 170°C for 10 minutes.
6. When done, the pudding should be just firm to the touch.
7. Serve at room temperature.

Pumpkin Pudding and Vanilla Wafers

Prep time: 10 minutes | Cook time: 15 minutes | Serves 4

- 1 cup tinned no-salt-added pumpkin purée (not pumpkin pie filling)
- ¼ cup packed Demerara sugar
- 3 tablespoons plain flour
- 1 egg, whisked
- 2 tablespoons milk
- 1 tablespoon unsalted butter, melted
- 1 teaspoon pure vanilla extract
- 4 low-fat vanilla wafers, crumbled
- Cooking spray

1. Coat a baking pan with cooking spray. Set aside.
2. Mix the pumpkin purée, Demerara sugar, flour, whisked egg, milk, melted butter, and vanilla in a medium bowl and whisk to combine. Transfer the mixture to the baking pan.
3. Slide the pan into the air fryer. Press the Power Button. Cook at 180°C for 15 minutes.
4. When cooking is complete, the pudding should be set.
5. Remove the pudding from the air fryer to a wire rack to cool.
6. Divide the pudding into four bowls and serve with the vanilla wafers sprinkled on top.

Strawberry and Rhubarb Crumble

Prep time: 10 minutes | Cook time: 12 to 17 minutes | Serves 6

- 1½ cups sliced fresh strawberries
- ⅓ cup sugar
- ¾ cup sliced rhubarb
- ⅔ cup quick-cooking Porridge
- ¼ cup packed Demerara sugar
- ½ cup whole-wheat soft flour
- ½ teaspoon ground cinnamon
- 3 tablespoons unsalted butter, melted

1. Place the strawberries, sugar, and rhubarb in a baking pan and toss to coat.
2. Combine the Porridge, Demerara sugar, soft flour, and cinnamon in a medium bowl.
3. Add the melted butter to the Porridge mixture and stir until crumbly. Sprinkle this generously on top of the strawberries and rhubarb.
4. Slide the pan into the air fryer. Press the Power Button. Cook at 190°C for 12 minutes.
5. Bake Cook until the fruit is bubbly and the topping is golden brown. Continue cooking for an additional 2 to 5 minutes if needed.
6. When cooking is complete, remove from the air fryer and serve warm.

Summer Berry Crisp

Prep time: 10 minutes | Cook time: 12 minutes | Serves 4

- ½ cup fresh blueberries
- ½ cup chopped fresh strawberries
- ⅓ cup frozen raspberries, thawed
- 1 tablespoon honey
- 1 tablespoon freshly squeezed lemon juice
- ⅔ cup whole-wheat soft flour
- 3 tablespoons packed Demerara sugar
- 2 tablespoons unsalted butter, melted

1. Place the blueberries, strawberries, and raspberries in a baking pan and drizzle the honey and lemon juice over the top.
2. Combine the soft flour and Demerara sugar in a small mixing bowl.
3. Add the butter and whisk until the mixture is crumbly. Scatter the flour mixture on top of the fruit.
4. Slide the pan into the air fryer. Press the Power Button. Cook at 190°C for 12 minutes.
5. When cooking is complete, the fruit should be bubbly and the topping should be golden brown.
6. Remove from the air fryer and serve on a plate.

Vanilla Chocolate Chip biscuits

Prep time: 10 minutes | Cook time: 22 minutes | Makes 30 biscuits

- ⅓ cup (80g) organic Demerara sugar
- ⅓ cup (80g) organic cane sugar
- 4 ounces (112g) cashew-based vegan butter
- ½ cup coconut cream
- 1 teaspoon vanilla extract
- 2 tablespoons ground flaxseed
- 1 teaspoon baking powder
- 1 teaspoon baking soda
- Pinch of salt
- 2¼ cups (220g) almond flour
- ½ cup (90g) dairy-free dark chocolate chips

1. Line a baking tray with greaseproof paper.
2. Mix the Demerara sugar, cane sugar, and butter in a medium bowl or the bowl of a stand mixer. Cream together with a mixer.
3. Fold in the coconut cream, vanilla, flaxseed, baking powder, baking soda, and salt. Stir well.
4. Add the almond flour, a little at a time, mixing after each addition until fully incorporated. Stir in the chocolate chips with a spatula.
5. Scoop the dough onto the prepared baking tray.
6. Slide the baking tray into the air fryer. Press the Power Button. Cook at 325°F (160°C) for 22 minutes.
7. Bake Cook until the biscuits are golden brown.
8. When cooking is complete, transfer the baking tray onto a wire rack to cool completely before serving.

Vanilla Walnuts Tart

Prep time: 5 minutes | Cook time: 13 minutes | Serves 6

- 1 cup coconut milk
- ½ cup walnuts, ground
- ½ cup Swerve
- ½ cup almond flour
- ½ stick butter, at room temperature
- 2 eggs
- 1 teaspoon vanilla essence
- ¼ teaspoon ground cardamom
- ¼ teaspoon ground cloves
- Cooking spray

1. Coat a baking pan with cooking spray.
2. Combine all the ingredients except the oil in a large bowl and stir until well blended. Spoon the batter mixture into the baking pan.
3. Slide the pan into the air fryer. Press the Power Button. Cook at 180°C for 13 minutes.
4. When cooking is complete, a toothpick inserted into the center of the tart should come out clean.
5. Remove from the air fryer and place on a wire rack to cool. Serve immediately.

Blackberry Pie

Prep time: 12 minutes | Cook time: 35 minutes | Serves 6

- ⅓ cup tapioca pearls
- 2 tablespoons sugar
- 4 cups blackberries
- 2 tablespoons soft butter
- 1 Digestive biscuits pie crust
- 1½ cups water

1. In a bowl, mix tapioca with sugar, blackberries and butter and whisk until sugar melts and pour the mixture into pie crust.
2. Add the water to the Instant Pot, arrange the steamer basket in the pot, then add the pie.
3. Lock the lid. Set the Instant Pot to Pressure Cook mode, then set the timer for 35 minutes at High Pressure.
4. When the timer goes off, perform a natural release for 10 minutes, then release any remaining pressure. Carefully open the lid.
5. Let the pie cool down, slice, divide between plates and serve.

Crispy Bananas

Prep time: 5 minutes | Cook time: 7 minutes | Serves 6

- 1 large egg
- ¼ cup cornflour
- ¼ cup plain bread crumbs
- 3 bananas, halved crosswise
- Cooking oil
- Chocolate sauce, for drizzling

1. In a small bowl, beat the egg. In another bowl, place the cornflour. Put the bread crumbs in a third bowl.
2. Dip the bananas in the cornflour, then the egg, and then the bread crumbs.
3. Spray the Duo Crisp basket with cooking oil.
4. Put the bananas in the air fryer basket or wire rack and spray them with cooking oil. Cook at the corresponding preset mode or Air Fry at 180°C for 7 minutes.
5. Transfer the bananas to plates. Drizzle the chocolate sauce over the bananas, and serve.

Peach, Plum, and Nectarine Skewers

Prep time: 10 minutes | Cook time: 3 to 5 minutes | Serves 4

- 2 peaches, peeled, pitted, and thickly sliced
- 3 plums, halved and pitted
- 3 nectarines, halved and pitted
- 1 tablespoon honey
- ½ teaspoon ground cinnamon
- ¼ teaspoon ground allspice
- Pinch cayenne pepper

SPECIAL EQUIPMENT:

- 8 metal skewers

7. Thread, alternating peaches, plums, and nectarines, onto the metal skewers that fit into the Duo Crisp.
8. Thoroughly combine the honey, cinnamon, allspice, and cayenne in a small bowl. Brush generously the glaze over the fruit skewers.
9. Transfer the fruit skewers to the Duo Crisp basket. You may need to cook in batches to avoid overcrowding.
10. Cook at the corresponding preset mode or Air Fry at 200°C for 3 to 5 minutes, or until the fruit is caramelized.
11. Remove from the air fryer basket or wire rack and repeat with the remaining fruit skewers.
12. Let the fruit skewers rest for 5 minutes before serving.

Baked Blueberries and Peaches

Prep time: 10 minutes | Cook time: 7 to 11 minutes | Serves 6

- 3 peaches, peeled, halved, and pitted
- 2 tablespoons packed Demerara sugar
- 1 cup plain Greek yogurt
- ¼ teaspoon ground cinnamon
- 1 teaspoon pure vanilla extract
- 1 cup fresh blueberries

1. Arrange the peaches in the Duo Crisp basket, cut-side up. Top with a generous sprinkle of Demerara sugar.
2. Cook at the corresponding preset mode or Air Fry at 190°C for 7 to 11 minutes, or until the peaches are lightly browned and caramelized.
3. Meanwhile, whisk together the yogurt, cinnamon, and vanilla in a small bowl until smooth.
4. Remove the peaches from the air fryer basket or wire rack to a plate. Serve topped with the yogurt mixture and fresh blueberries.

Peach and Apple Crumble

Prep time: 10 minutes | Cook time: 10 to 12 minutes | Serves 4

- 2 peaches, peeled, pitted, and chopped
- 1 apple, peeled and chopped
- 2 tablespoons honey
- ½ cup quick-cooking Porridge
- ⅓ cup whole-wheat soft flour
- 2 tablespoons unsalted butter, at room temperature
- 3 tablespoons packed Demerara sugar
- ½ teaspoon ground cinnamon

1. Mix together the peaches, apple, and honey in a nonstick round baking pan until well incorporated.
2. In a bowl, combine the Porridge, soft flour, butter, Demerara sugar, and cinnamon and stir to mix well. Spread this mixture evenly over the fruit.
3. Detach the rotating blade of the Duo Crisp basket. Place the baking pan in the Duo Crisp basket and cook at the corresponding preset mode or Bake at 190°C for 10 to 12 minutes, or until the fruit is bubbling around the edges and the topping is golden brown.
4. Remove from the air fryer basket or wire rack and serve warm.

Appendix 1 Measurement Conversion Chart

Volume Equivalents (Dry)	
US STANDARD	METRIC (APPROXIMATE)
1/8 teaspoon	0.5 mL
1/4 teaspoon	1 mL
1/2 teaspoon	2 mL
3/4 teaspoon	4 mL
1 teaspoon	5 mL
1 tablespoon	15 mL
1/4 cup	59 mL
1/2 cup	118 mL
3/4 cup	177 mL
1 cup	235 mL
2 cups	475 mL
3 cups	700 mL
4 cups	1 L

Volume Equivalents (Liquid)		
US STANDARD	US STANDARD (OUNCES)	METRIC (APPROXIMATE)
2 tablespoons	1 fl.oz.	30 mL
1/4 cup	2 fl.oz.	60 mL
1/2 cup	4 fl.oz.	120 mL
1 cup	8 fl.oz.	240 mL
1 1/2 cup	12 fl.oz.	355 mL
2 cups or 1 pint	16 fl.oz.	475 mL
4 cups or 1 quart	32 fl.oz.	1 L
1 gallon	128 fl.oz.	4 L

Weight Equivalents	
US STANDARD	METRIC (APPROXIMATE)
1 ounce	28 g
2 ounces	57 g
5 ounces	142 g
10 ounces	284 g
15 ounces	425 g
16 ounces (1 pound)	455 g
1.5 pounds	680 g
2 pounds	907 g

Temperatures Equivalents	
FAHRENHEIT(F)	CELSIUS(C) APPROXIMATE)
225 °F	107 °C
250 °F	120 ° °C
275 °F	135 °C
300 °F	150 °C
325 °F	160 °C
350 °F	180 °C
375 °F	190 °C
400 °F	205 °C
425 °F	220 °C
450 °F	235 °C
475 °F	245 °C
500 °F	260 °C

Appendix 2 The Dirty Dozen and Clean Fifteen

The Environmental Working Group (EWG) is a nonprofit, nonpartisan organization dedicated to protecting human health and the environment Its mission is to empower people to live healthier lives in a healthier environment. This organization publishes an annual list of the twelve kinds of produce, in sequence, that have the highest amount of pesticide residue-the Dirty Dozen-as well as a list of the fifteen kinds of produce that have the least amount of pesticide residue-the Clean Fifteen.

THE DIRTY DOZEN

The 2016 Dirty Dozen includes the following produce. These are considered among the year's most important produce to buy organic:

Strawberries	Spinach
Apples	Tomatoes
Nectarines	Bell peppers
Peaches	Cherry tomatoes
Celery	Cucumbers
Grapes	Kale/collard greens
Cherries	Hot peppers

The Dirty Dozen list contains two additional items—kale/collard greens and hot peppers—because they tend to contain trace levels of highly hazardous pesticides.

THE CLEAN FIFTEEN

The least critical to buy organically are the Clean Fifteen list. The following are on the 2016 list:

Avocados	Papayas
Corn	Kiw
Pineapples	Eggplant
Cabbage	Honeydew
Sweet peas	Grapefruit
Onions	Cantaloupe
Asparagus	Cauliflower
Mangos	

Some of the sweet corn sold in the United States are made from genetically engineered (GE) seedstock. Buy organic varieties of these crops to avoid GE produce.

Appendix 3 Index

A
almond flour 25
apple cider vinegar 24
asparagus 30
avocado 24, 25, 26, 27, 28, 30
avocado oil 24, 25, 26, 27, 28, 30

B
butter 31

C
cauliflower 31
cayenne pepper 26
chicken 24, 25, 26, 27, 28, 29, 30, 31
chicken breasts 26
chicken drumsticks 28
chicken stock 26
chicken thighs 31
chicken wings 25, 27, 28, 29
chili flakes 26, 28
chili pepper 26
coconut 24, 25, 26, 29, 30, 31
coconut aminos 26
coconut cream 31
coconut oil 24, 25, 29, 30
coriander 28, 29
Cornish hens 24

D
dried basil 27
dried dill 26
dried oregano 28

E
egg 26
Erythritol 25, 26

G
Gai yang spices 24
garlic 28, 29, 31
garlic powder 28, 29
ginger 26
ground cumin 28

K
keto BBQ sauce 28

L
lemon 27, 28, 29
lemon juice 27, 28
lemon zest 27, 28

N
nutmeg 30

O
olive oil 26, 28, 29, 31
onion 26, 30
onion powder 26, 30

P
paprika 24, 26, 30
Parmesan 26
parsley 31
pork 26
pork rinds 26

S
scallions 30
stevia 26

T
taco seasoning 25
thyme 31

ASHLEY C. SPRADLIN

Printed in Great Britain
by Amazon

15872666R00054